MASTERING

QUICKEN

"A Comprehensive Guide for Beginners and Pros:
Simplify Budgeting, Expense Tracking, and Financial
Planning"

BY

REBECCA B. FORD

COPYRIGHT @ 2025. ALL RIGHTS RESERVED

REBECCA B. FORD

DISCLAIMER

This book is an independent guide and is not affiliated with, endorsed by, or sponsored by Quicken Inc. All product names, trademarks, and registered trademarks are the property of their respective owners. The information provided is for educational purposes only and is based on the author's experience and research. Readers are advised to refer to the official Quicken documentation for additional guidance.

TABLE OF CONTENTS

Contents

INTRODUCTION

Managing money is one of the most crucial life skills, yet it's something many of us struggle with. Whether you're just starting out on your financial journey or looking for better ways to organize your expenses, there's one undeniable truth: financial chaos leads to stress, missed opportunities, and a lack of control. But what if there was a way to make money management simple, streamlined, and even empowering?

That's where Quicken comes in. For decades, this trusted financial tool has helped individuals and businesses alike take charge of their money. From basic budgeting to advanced financial planning, Quicken has proven to be a game-changer for those who want to regain control over their finances.

This book, *Mastering Quicken: A Comprehensive Guide for Beginners and Pros*, is your ultimate roadmap to harnessing the full power of Quicken. Whether you're completely new to personal finance or a seasoned user aiming to unlock its advanced features, this guide will meet you where you are and help you achieve your financial goals.

Inside, you'll discover how to:

- Set up Quicken to fit your unique financial needs.

- Track every dollar with ease and clarity.

- Create customized budgets that actually work.

- Monitor expenses and spot areas where you can save more.

- Plan for the future with confidence, from saving for a dream vacation to preparing for retirement.

- Use advanced tools to manage investments, loans, and even business finances.

Beyond the technical how-to, this book is packed with practical tips, relatable examples, and actionable advice to help you transform the way you manage money. By the time you finish reading, you won't just know how to use Quicken—you'll have the confidence to make informed financial decisions and build the life you want.

CHAPTER ONE: QUICKEN 101

Managing your personal finances can often feel like trying to solve a puzzle without all the pieces. Bills pile up, budgets go off track, and tracking expenses can become a juggling act. That's where Quicken comes in—a powerful yet user-friendly tool designed to simplify the chaos and put you back in control. But where do you start? Quicken 101 is your go-to guide for navigating this versatile financial software. Whether you're a complete beginner or someone looking to unlock its full potential, this introduction lays the foundation for understanding how Quicken can transform the way you manage money.

From setting up accounts and tracking expenses to creating budgets and running insightful reports, Quicken offers a comprehensive toolkit to help you organize your finances with confidence. This section will cover the basics in plain, straightforward terms, breaking down what Quicken is, how it works, and why it's a game-changer for so many users. By the end of this introduction, you'll not only understand the core functions of Quicken but also see how it can fit seamlessly into your life, helping you achieve your financial goals with ease. Let's take that first step together and unlock the potential of Quicken!

What Exactly is a Quicken?

Quicken is a powerful personal finance software designed to help you track income, expenses, budgets, and even investments. Whether you're managing household finances or running a small business, Quicken provides tools to ensure you have a clear picture of your financial situation at all times. The software is available in different versions to meet specific needs, including Quicken Starter, Quicken Deluxe, Quicken Premier, and Quicken Home & Business. Each version adds extra features to help you gain more control and insight over your finances, making it essential for both beginners and advanced users.

Who is This Particular Book Meant For

This book is written for individuals at all levels of financial experience. Whether you're new to finance management or you're a small business owner looking for a better way to track expenses and income, you'll find everything you need here. It's also ideal for those who may already be using Quicken but are looking to dive deeper into its features to maximize its potential. Throughout the book, you'll learn how to:

- Set up and manage your bank accounts within Quicken.
- Track your spending and income effortlessly.
- Create and follow a budget that keeps you on track.
- Use Quickens investment tracking tools to manage and grow your portfolio.
- Prepare for taxes by organizing your deductible expenses.

How to Use this Book

This book is designed to be your step-by-step companion as you learn to navigate Quicken and take control of your finances. Whether you're a complete beginner or have some experience with the software, you'll find practical advice, clear instructions, and helpful tips to make your learning process smooth and effective.

Here's how to make the most of this guide:

1. **Start with the Basics**: If you're new to Quicken, begin with the foundational chapters. These sections will introduce you to the software, its key features, and how to set it up for your personal financial needs.

2. **Follow Step-by-Step Instructions**: Each chapter builds on the previous one, offering detailed walkthroughs for specific tasks like budgeting, tracking expenses, and generating reports. Follow the steps as you go, and don't hesitate to pause and practice within your Quicken software.

3. **Use It as a Reference**: Already familiar with certain features? Feel free to jump to the sections that interest you most. This book is organized for easy navigation, so you can quickly find the answers you're looking for.

4. **Take Notes and Experiment**: Quicken is a powerful tool, and the more you explore, the more comfortable you'll become. Jot down your own insights, customize settings, and experiment with the features to see what works best for you.

Remember, this book is here to guide you, not overwhelm you. Take your time, enjoy the learning process, and watch as Quicken helps you transform your financial management. Let's get started!

CHAPTER TWO: STARTING YOUR QUICKEN JOURNEY

Every journey begins with a single step, and your path to mastering personal finance starts here. Whether you're feeling overwhelmed by budgeting, struggling to keep track of expenses, or simply searching for a better way to organize your money, you've made the right choice with Quicken. Think of this book as your personal roadmap—a guide to navigating the sometimes-daunting world of financial management with clarity and confidence. Along the way, you'll learn how to use Quicken not just as a tool but as a trusted ally in building a more secure financial future.

Starting with the basics, you'll uncover how to set up your accounts, categorize your spending, and monitor your financial health—all at your own pace. As you move forward, we'll dive into more advanced features, from creating budgets and running reports to forecasting for the future. This isn't just about software; it's about empowerment. By embarking on this journey, you're taking a proactive step toward financial control, turning what once felt like a chore into a rewarding process. So, buckle up, open your Quicken app, and get ready to explore a world where managing money becomes second nature. Your financial transformation starts now—let's begin this journey together!

Selecting the Appropriate Quicken Version

When it comes to selecting the right Quicken version for your needs, it's essential to understand that each version is designed with specific features and functions to cater to different financial situations. Quicken offers several versions, ranging from basic personal finance tools to advanced business management features. Choosing the right version depends on your individual or business financial needs. Choosing the right Quicken version is crucial for maximizing your financial management experience. Quicken offers several editions tailored to different needs:

- **Quicken Starter:** Ideal for beginners, focusing on basic budgeting and expense tracking.

- **Quicken Deluxe:** Perfect for users wanting to create custom budgets and track savings goals.

- **Quicken Premier:** Best for those who need advanced investment tracking and insights.

- **Quicken Home & Business:** Designed for individuals managing both personal and small business finances.

Consider your financial goals and the features you need to make an informed choice that aligns with your lifestyle.

Quicken Starter

If you are new to personal finance software and simply need basic tools to track your income, expenses, and budgeting, Quicken Starter is a great option. This version is designed for individuals who are primarily focused on managing everyday financial activities like paying bills, tracking spending, and creating simple budgets. It allows users to link bank accounts, categorize expenses, and get a clear picture of their cash flow without diving into advanced features. However, it lacks tools for investment tracking and more complex financial planning, making it a good choice for someone just starting on their financial journey.

Key Features

- Track income and expenses.
- Simple budgeting tools.
- Link bank accounts and categorize transactions.

Quicken Deluxe

For users looking to go beyond basic financial management, Quicken Deluxe adds several essential features. In addition to tracking income and expenses, Deluxe helps you plan for future financial goals, such as saving for a down payment or a vacation. It also introduces tools for managing loans and debt, making it easier to reduce debt and improve your financial standing over time. This version is ideal for individuals who want a more comprehensive view of their finances without delving into advanced investment features.

Key Features

- All features of Quicken Starter.
- Loan tracking and debt reduction tools.
- Enhanced budgeting options for future financial planning.
- Allows customization of categories and reports.

Quicken Premier

If you have investments or retirement accounts to manage, Quicken Premier is a step up from Deluxe. Premier includes everything in Deluxe but offers more robust tools for tracking your investments. You can link brokerage accounts, track the performance of your investment portfolio, and generate reports that help you analyse your financial position in detail. Premier also comes with tax-planning tools, including features that help you identify deductible expenses and maximize your returns.

Key Features

- All features of Quicken Deluxe.
- Investment tracking, including stocks, bonds, and mutual funds.
- Advanced reports for investment performance and portfolio analysis.
- Tax planning tools to track deductible expenses.

Quicken Home & Business

For small business owners or freelancers, Quicken Home & Business offers comprehensive tools that combine both personal and business finance management. This version includes everything from Quicken Premier, plus features specific to business finances. You can track business income and expenses separately, create and send invoices, and generate business-specific reports like profit and loss statements. Additionally, this version is useful for managing rental properties, with features for tracking tenants, rental income, and related expenses.

Key Features

- All features of Quicken Premier.

- Tools for invoicing and payment tracking.
- Profit and loss reporting for businesses.
- Rental property management tools.

Quicken for Mac

For users on macOS, Quicken for Mac provides a similar experience to the Windows versions, with slight variations in the interface. It covers the same core features as Quicken Deluxe, including budgeting, bill tracking, and investment management, but users may notice that certain advanced features from Premier and Home & Business are more limited. Nonetheless, it remains a robust option for Mac users who need to keep track of their finances efficiently.

Key Features

- Track income, expenses, and budgets.
- Basic investment tracking.
- Similar functionality to Quicken Deluxe on Windows, with a Mac-friendly interface.

Which Version is Right for You?

Choosing the right version depends on the complexity of your financial needs. If you're just starting out and need basic budget tracking, Quicken Starter is likely sufficient. For users who want more comprehensive tools for managing loans, budgets, and long-term financial goals, Quicken Deluxe provides the perfect balance of features. Investors and those who need detailed portfolio management should opt for Quicken Premier, while small business owners will benefit from the advanced tools in Quicken Home & Business. For Mac users, Quicken for Mac provides a streamlined experience with essential features, select the version that best aligns with your current financial situation and future goals. Each version of Quicken is designed to make your financial management process more efficient, so you can take control of your finances with confidence.

Quicken download and installation

Once you've chosen the right version of Quicken for your needs, the next step is downloading and installing the software. Whether you're using Windows or Mac, the process is straightforward, but there are slight differences in installation depending on your operating system. Getting started with Quicken is simple and straightforward. To begin, visit the official Quicken website and choose the version that best suits your financial needs. Once you've made your selection, click on the download link to initiate the installation process. Follow the prompts to install the software on your computer, ensuring you have a stable internet connection throughout. After installation, launch Quicken, and you'll be guided through the setup process to create your account and personalize your financial dashboard. With just a few easy steps, you'll be ready to take control of your finances!

Downloading Quicken

For Windows Users:

1. **Purchase Quicken:** First, visit the official Quicken website and select the version that suits your needs. After purchasing, you'll receive a confirmation email containing a download link and your license information.

2. **Create or log in to Your Quicken Account:** If you already have a Quicken account, sign in with your credentials. If not, create a new account using your email address. This account is necessary for managing your license and syncing data across devices.

3. **Download the Software:** Once logged in, go to your account dashboard and select "Download Quicken" under your purchased products. Click the download link for the Windows version.

For Mac Users:

1. **Visit the Quicken Website:** Navigate to the official Quicken website and choose the version compatible with macOS. Just like for Windows, complete your purchase and check your email for a download link.

2. **Download Quicken for Mac:** After signing in to your Quicken account, select "Download" from your account dashboard. Ensure you choose the version labelled for macOS.

Installing Quicken

For Windows Users:

1. **Locate the Downloaded File:** Once the download is complete, locate the installer file in your Downloads folder or wherever your browser saves downloaded files. The file name will usually be something like "Quicken.exe."

2. **Run the Installer:** Double-click the downloaded file to begin the installation process. Windows may ask for confirmation to allow the program to make changes—click "Yes" to proceed.

3. **Follow the On-Screen Instructions:** The Quicken installer will guide you through the setup process. You'll be prompted to accept the license agreement and choose an installation folder. It's recommended to leave the default settings unless you have a specific reason to change them.

4. **Enter Your License Information:** After installation, you will be asked to enter the license code you received in your confirmation email. This step is crucial to activate the software.

5. **Finish the Installation:** Once the installation is complete, Quicken will prompt you to open the application. You can choose to launch it immediately or at a later time.

For Mac Users:

1. **Locate the Downloaded File:** Once the download finishes, find the installer file in your Downloads folder or your designated download location. The file will have a ".dmg" extension, such as "Quicken.dmg."

2. **Run the Installer:** Double-click the ".dmg" file to open the installation window. You'll see a Quicken icon and a prompt to drag the icon into your Applications folder.

3. **Drag Quicken to Applications:** Drag the Quicken icon into the Applications folder, which installs the software on your Mac.

4. **Open Quicken:** Once installed, open the Quicken application from your Applications folder. The system may ask for permission to run the program since it was downloaded from the internet—click "Open" to continue.

5. **Sign in with Your Quicken ID:** After launching Quicken, you will be prompted to sign in with your Quicken ID. Use the email and password you created when you purchased the software.

Configuring Updates Automatically

Quicken frequently releases updates to improve performance, fix bugs, and add new features. After installation, it's recommended to enable automatic updates, so you always have the latest version of the software.

For Windows Users:

Quicken typically enables automatic updates during installation. However, you can check by going to the "Help" menu in the Quicken interface and selecting "Check for Updates". If a newer version is available, follow the prompts to install it.

For Mac Users:

Mac users can similarly check for updates by going to the "Quicken" menu and selecting "Check for Updates". Enabling automatic updates ensures you stay up to date with the latest features.

Logging in and Making the First Setup

After the installation is complete and you've launched the software, you'll need to sign in with your Quicken ID. This ID is linked to your license and ensures that your data is securely synced across devices, if applicable. If this is your first time using Quicken, you'll also be prompted to complete the initial setup, including linking bank accounts and setting preferences, which will be covered in the next chapter.

Creating an Account on Quicken

Once you have successfully downloaded and installed Quicken, the next step is to set up your Quicken account. This process allows you to link your financial accounts, customize your preferences, and start tracking your income and expenses. Whether you are using Quicken for personal finances or small business management, setting up your account correctly is essential to make the most of the software's features. Below is a detailed, step-by-step guide on how to set up your Quicken account.

Creating an account or logging in with your Quicken ID

The first thing you'll need to do when you open Quicken for the first time is sign in with your Quicken ID. If you've used Quicken before, simply log in using your existing credentials. If you're new to Quicken, you will need to create an account.

For New Users:

1. **Open Quicken:** After installation, launch the Quicken application from your desktop (Windows) or Applications folder (Mac).

2. **Create Quicken ID:** When prompted, click "Create Account" or "Sign Up" to begin. You'll need to provide some basic information, such as your email address, a password, and your country of residence.

3. **Verify Your Email:** Once you've entered your details, Quicken will send a verification email to the address you provided. Check your inbox, open the email, and click the verification link to confirm your account.

4. **Complete Registration:** After verifying your email, return to Quicken and complete the registration process. You will be prompted to enter additional details like your name and preferences.

For Returning Users:

1. **Sign In with Quicken ID:** If you already have a Quicken ID, simply click "Sign In" and enter your email and password.

2. **Sync with Existing Data:** If you have used Quicken on another device or have cloud data from a previous version, Quicken will offer to sync this data to your current installation. If you want to start fresh, you can skip this step and begin setting up new accounts.

Choosing Your Preferences

Once you've logged in, it's important to customize Quickens settings according to your personal needs. Setting the right preferences will ensure that Quicken operates the way you want and displays relevant financial data.

Currency and Region Settings:

- Quicken will automatically detect your region based on your registration details, but you can manually adjust these settings if necessary.
- Go to the Edit > Preferences (Windows) or Quicken > Preferences (Mac) menu to change your default currency or adjust the time zone.

Choosing Your Startup View:

- Quicken lets you decide what screen you see when the software opens. For instance, you may want to view your "Dashboard" with an overview of your accounts, or you may prefer to go straight to your "Transactions" page.
- To set your startup view, go to "Preferences" and select the desired default screen.

Customizing Categories and Tags:

- Quicken automatically comes with a list of pre-set categories such as "Groceries," "Rent," or "Utilities." However, you can add or customize categories to fit your specific financial situation.
- You can also create tags to add additional layers of organization. For example, if you want to track vacation-related expenses across different categories, you can create a "Vacation" tag and apply it to all related transactions.

Including Your Bank Accounts

After setting your preferences, the next step is to add your financial accounts to Quicken. The software allows you to link your bank accounts, credit cards, loans, investments, and even cash accounts to track every aspect of your finances in one place.

Step 1

Navigating to the Add Account Section:

- From the Quicken main screen, click "Add Account" in the top menu bar or in the left-hand panel. This will open a window that displays a list of different types of accounts you can add.
- Choose the type of account you want to add (e.g., checking, savings, credit card, or investment).

Step 2

Connecting to Your Bank:

- Find Your Bank: Quicken has a list of supported financial institutions. Start typing the name of your bank and select it from the list.

- Log In to Your Bank Account: Quicken will prompt you to log in using your online banking credentials. This process is secure and Quicken uses encryption to protect your information.

- Syncing Transactions: Once your bank account is connected, Quicken will automatically download your most recent transactions. The first download typically includes the past 90 days of transactions, but this may vary depending on your bank.

Step 3

Adding Manual Accounts:

- If your financial institution isn't supported or if you want to track accounts manually (such as cash or loans that aren't linked to a bank), you can add a manual account. To do this, select "Manual Entry" when adding a new account.

- Enter the account balance and other relevant details such as account type and currency. You will need to update these accounts manually as transactions occur.

Connecting to Quicken Cloud

Quicken offers the option to sync your data with the Quicken Cloud, allowing you to access your financial information from multiple devices, including smartphones and tablets. If you plan to manage your finances on the go or across multiple platforms, syncing with the cloud can be a useful feature.

How to Enable Cloud Sync:

- From the main menu, go to "Mobile & Web" and select "Sync Now".
- Follow the on-screen instructions to set up cloud sync.
- Quicken will automatically update your data to the cloud after this setup. You can access your financial information through the Quicken mobile app or web interface.

Finalizing Your Setup

Once your accounts are linked and your preferences are set, Quicken will begin tracking your transactions and financial activity. You'll have access to a detailed overview of your finances, with charts, graphs, and reports that provide valuable insights into your spending, income, and net worth.

- **Check Your Dashboard:** The dashboard gives you a summary of your financial health, including balances, upcoming bills, and recent transactions. Customize this view to focus on the areas that are most important to you.
- **Review Your Linked Accounts:** Make sure all your accounts are correctly linked and that the balances match what you have in your bank or financial institution.
- **Set Up a Backup Schedule:** To avoid losing data, set up regular backups by going to "File > Backup and Restore". Quicken can store backups locally or in the cloud for added security.

Getting Around the Quickens Interface

Once your Quicken account is set up and your financial accounts are linked, the next crucial step is to familiarize yourself with Quickens interface. Understanding how to navigate the various sections and features of the software will help you use Quicken efficiently and make the most of its capabilities. This guide will walk you through Quickens interface, explaining key sections and customization options to tailor the software to your specific needs.

The Main Dashboard

The "Dashboard" is the first screen you'll encounter when opening Quicken. It provides an overview of your financial situation, displaying key information like account balances, upcoming bills, recent transactions, and a summary of your spending.

Key Features of the Dashboard:

- Account Balances: A quick summary of the balances for your checking, savings, credit card, loan, and investment accounts. This section allows you to see all your accounts in one place without navigating to each individually.

- Upcoming Bills and Income: Displays your scheduled bill payments, expected income, and any recurring transactions you've set up. This is especially useful for ensuring you stay on top of your financial obligations.

- Spending Overview: This feature shows a breakdown of your spending by category (e.g., groceries, utilities, entertainment) so you can quickly see where your money is going.

- Net Worth Summary: Quicken calculates your net worth based on the total value of your assets (e.g., cash, investments) minus your liabilities (e.g., loans, credit card debt). This gives you a snapshot of your overall financial health.

Customizing the Dashboard:

- You can personalize your dashboard to focus on the financial information that matters most to you. Simply click on the gear icon (usually in the top-right corner of the Dashboard) and select the data you want to display.
- Add, remove, or rearrange sections such as account balances, spending categories, and upcoming bills to prioritize the information that's most relevant.

The Left Panel: Accounts and Navigation

The left-hand panel is the central navigation hub in Quicken. It provides easy access to all your accounts and other financial information. Understanding how to navigate this panel will save you time and make managing your finances more straightforward.

Key Sections of the Left Panel:

- Banking: This section displays all your checking and savings accounts. Clicking on any account will show you the transactions associated with it, as well as your current balance.
- Credit Cards: All your linked credit cards will appear here. By clicking on a specific credit card, you can review transactions, payments, and outstanding balances.

- Investing: If you've linked any brokerage or retirement accounts, they will appear under this section. You can track your portfolio's performance and see individual investments like stocks, bonds, or mutual funds.

- Property & Debt: This section tracks your assets (like real estate or vehicles) and liabilities (such as mortgages, loans, or credit card debt). You can view payment schedules and loan balances.

- Budgeting & Goals: From here, you can create and manage budgets, track your spending against your financial goals, and set alerts for when you're nearing budget limits.

Navigating Between Accounts:

- Clicking on any of the accounts listed in the left panel will take you directly to that account's "Transaction Register", where you can view and edit individual transactions.

- The panel also includes quick links to common actions such as "Add Account" or "Create Invoice" (for business users), making it easy to perform frequently used tasks.

The Toolbar: Easy Access to Important Functions

At the top of the screen, you'll find Quickens toolbar, which provides quick access to essential features and settings. The toolbar's layout may vary slightly between Windows and Mac versions, but the core functions remain the same.

Key Buttons on the Toolbar:

- **Add Account:** Allows you to add new bank accounts, credit cards, loans, or investment accounts. You can also use this button to set up manual accounts that are not linked to financial institutions.

- **Reports:** Generates various financial reports, including spending summaries, income statements, and net worth reports. You can also create custom reports to track specific financial goals or account activity.

- **Mobile & Web Sync:** If you've set up cloud syncing, this button will sync your desktop data with the Quicken cloud, ensuring your data is up to date on all devices.

- **Calendar:** Opens a visual representation of your financial activities, including bill due dates, scheduled transactions, and income reminders. This is a helpful tool for planning and staying organized.

- **Search Bar:** Located at the top-right corner of the toolbar, the search bar allows you to quickly locate transactions, accounts, or reports by typing in keywords.

Viewing and Managing Transactions with the Transaction Register

Each account in Quicken has its own "Transaction Register", where all the activity related to that account is listed. This register functions similarly to a traditional check book register, but with added features for sorting, filtering, and categorizing transactions.

Key Features of the Transaction Register:

- **Transaction Details:** Each entry in the register includes the date, payee, category, tags, amount, and balance after the transaction. You can manually edit any of these fields by clicking on the specific transaction.

- **Categorization:** Quicken automatically assigns categories to transactions (e.g., "Dining," "Utilities"), but you can manually change these if needed. Proper categorization is essential for accurate budgeting and reporting.

- **Sorting & Filtering:** Use the sort and filter options to organize transactions by date, amount, category, or payee. Filtering options allow you to view only certain types of transactions (e.g., only expenses or only income).

- **Splitting Transactions:** For complex purchases that involve multiple categories (e.g., a shopping trip where you buy groceries, clothing, and household items), Quicken allows you to split a single transaction into multiple categories for better tracking.

Reports & Analysis: Understanding Your Financial Situation

Quickens reporting tools allow you to analyse your financial data and track your progress toward financial goals. These reports provide in-depth insights into various aspects of your finances, helping you make informed decisions.

Generating Reports:

- To access reports, click on the "Reports" button in the toolbar. From here, you can select from a variety of pre-built reports, such as "Spending by Category", "Income vs. Expenses", or "Net Worth".

- Reports are fully customizable. You can adjust the date range, account type, and categories to fit your specific needs.

Customizing Reports:

- For those looking to track specific financial data, Quicken offers the ability to create custom reports. You can define the parameters, such as which accounts to include or which types of transactions to analyse.
- Custom reports can be saved for future use, making it easy to generate regular financial updates or reviews.

Calendar: Monitoring Your Budgetary Timetable

The "Calendar" tool in Quicken is a visual representation of your financial activity. It shows upcoming bill payments, recurring transactions, and income, giving you a clear overview of what's coming up and helping you plan accordingly.

Key Features of the Calendar:

- **Bill Reminders:** Displays due dates for upcoming bills, ensuring you never miss a payment.
- **Scheduled Transactions:** Lists recurring transactions like pay checks, mortgage payments, or monthly subscriptions.
- **Income and Expense View:** Provides an overview of your expected cash flow on specific days, helping you anticipate periods where expenses may exceed income.

CHAPTER THREE: CONFIGURING YOUR ACCOUNT

Embarking on your financial management journey with Quicken is an exciting step toward achieving your money goals, but before you dive into budgeting and expense tracking, you need to get the software up and running. Thankfully, the process of downloading and installing Quicken is designed to be user-friendly, ensuring that you can start managing your finances without unnecessary hassle. Whether you're a seasoned finance pro or a newcomer looking to take control of your budgeting, the first step is to visit the official Quicken website. This introduction to Quicken sets the stage for your financial transformation. Let's dive into the details of downloading and installing Quicken, so you can begin harnessing the power of this versatile tool to achieve your financial aspirations!

Step One: Connecting Your Bank Accounts

One of the most powerful features of Quicken is its ability to link directly to your financial accounts, allowing you to automatically import transactions and track your finances in real-time. By linking your bank accounts, credit cards, loans, and even investment accounts, you can ensure that all your financial information is centralized and up-to-date. This step-by-step guide will walk you through how to securely link your bank accounts to Quicken, ensuring a seamless integration.

Accessing the Add Account Function

After you've logged in to your Quicken account, the first step to linking your bank accounts is to navigate to the "Add Account" option. This can be easily accessed from multiple places within the Quicken interface:

- **From the Main Dashboard:** On the left panel, there is an option to "Add Account" at the top. Clicking this will initiate the process.
- **From the Toolbar:** At the top of the screen, there's also an "Add Account" button that serves the same function.

When you click on "Add Account", a window will pop up, asking you to select the type of account you want to add. This step is crucial because Quicken supports a wide range of account types, and you'll need to select the correct one for proper tracking.

Selecting the Type of Account

Quicken allows you to link various types of financial accounts, ensuring comprehensive tracking. When prompted, choose the appropriate account type from the following list:

- Banking (Checking, Savings): These are your standard accounts for everyday transactions.
- Credit Cards: If you want to track your credit card spending and balances.
- Loan Accounts: For mortgages, auto loans, student loans, and other debt.
- Investing: Brokerage accounts, retirement accounts (IRA, 401k), and other investment portfolios.

- Cash Accounts: For tracking cash transactions manually, without a linked institution.

Finding and Selecting Your Bank

Once you've chosen the account type (e.g., Checking or Savings), Quicken will prompt you to find your bank or financial institution. Quicken has a built-in list of supported institutions, which includes most major banks and credit unions.

- **Search for Your Bank:** Start typing the name of your financial institution in the search bar. Quicken will automatically provide suggestions as you type. Select your bank from the list once it appears.
- **Unsupported Banks:** If your bank is not supported, you will be given the option to enter your account details manually, but this means you won't be able to download transactions automatically.

Entering the Login Information for Your Bank

After selecting your bank, Quicken will ask you to enter your online banking credentials. This typically includes your username and password, just like when logging in to your bank's website. Quicken uses secure encryption protocols to ensure your information is safe and protected.

Security Note:

Quicken employs bank-level security encryption (256-bit encryption) to protect your login credentials. Your information is stored securely and Quicken only uses it to download your financial data. It's also worth noting that Quicken does not have the ability to move money between your accounts—its role is strictly to view and categorize transactions.

Selecting Accounts to Link

After successful authentication, Quicken will display a list of accounts available for linking. These could include:

- Checking accounts
- Savings accounts
- Credit cards
- Loans
- Investment accounts

Choose which accounts you'd like to link to Quicken by selecting the checkboxes next to each one. You can link as many or as few accounts as you wish. Once you've made your selection, click "Next" to continue.

Downloading Transactions

Once you've linked your accounts, Quicken will start downloading your transaction history. For most banks, Quicken will pull transactions from the past 90 days. However, this period may vary depending on your bank's policies and the type of account you've linked.

Initial Download: During this first download, it may take a few minutes for all transactions to be imported, especially if you have a large volume of transactions or multiple accounts linked. You can monitor progress on the screen and Quicken will notify you once it's done.

Categorizing Transactions

After downloading your transactions, Quicken will automatically categorize them based on the payee or merchant information. For example, a grocery store purchase may be categorized as "Groceries," while a restaurant transaction may be labelled as "Dining."

- Review and Edit Categories: It's important to review these categories to ensure accuracy, as some transactions may not be categorized correctly. You can manually change categories by clicking on the transaction and selecting a new category from the drop-down list.

- Creating Custom Categories: If you want more specific categories (e.g., "Online Shopping" or "Business Travel"), Quicken allows you to create custom categories tailored to your needs. This feature helps you track spending more accurately.

Setting Up Account Preferences

Once your transactions are categorized, take a moment to customize your account settings. In the account preferences section, you can:

- **Set Alerts:** Choose to receive notifications for low balances, large transactions, or upcoming bills.

- **Automatic Updates:** Enable automatic transaction downloads, so Quicken syncs with your bank on a regular basis without manual intervention.

- **Reconcile Accounts:** Set up monthly reconciliation for checking and credit card accounts to ensure your Quicken records match your bank statements.

Troubleshooting and Syncing Issues

In some cases, you may encounter problems while linking your bank accounts, such as syncing errors or incorrect balances. Here are a few common issues and solutions:

- **Sync Errors:** If Quicken is unable to sync with your bank, try refreshing the connection by clicking the "Update" button in the toolbar. You may also need to log out and log back into Quicken.
- **Duplicate Transactions:** If you notice duplicate entries, Quicken provides tools to merge or delete them.
- **Account Not Syncing:** Some banks may temporarily disable third-party access. If this happens, contact your bank's customer service to confirm if the issue is on their end.

Step Two: Including Manual Accounts

While Quicken makes it easy to link many financial institutions for automatic transaction downloads, there are times when you may need to manually add accounts. This could be because your bank or financial institution isn't supported by Quicken or if you have other types of accounts—such as cash, investments, or loans—that you want to track manually. Manually adding accounts ensures that all of your finances, even those that cannot be linked electronically, are accounted for in Quicken. Below is a step-by-step guide on how to manually add and manage accounts in Quicken.

How to Add an Account

To manually add an account, start by navigating to the "Add Account" option in Quickens interface:

- From the Dashboard: Look for the "Add Account" button, typically located on the left-hand side of the screen or at the top of the toolbar.
- From the Left Panel: You can also access the "Add Account" option through the left-hand panel by selecting the specific section where the account fits (e.g., Banking, Loans, Investments).
- Once you click "Add Account", a window will pop up asking you to select the type of account you want to add. Since you'll be entering this information manually, the steps will differ slightly from linking a bank account.

The Process of Adding an Account

Just like when linking a bank account, Quicken will prompt you to select the type of account you want to add. Here are some of the common types of accounts you might add manually:

- **Checking or Savings Accounts:** If you prefer to track these accounts manually or if your bank doesn't allow third-party integration.
- **Cash Accounts:** To track day-to-day cash expenditures, you can create a separate cash account.

- **Loans or Debts:** If you have loans (such as a mortgage or student loan) that aren't automatically linked, you can track them manually by adding the loan details.

- **Investment Accounts:** For brokerage or retirement accounts that you want to track without automatic syncing.

After selecting the appropriate account type, Quicken will direct you to manually input the details of that account.

Inputting Account Details

Once you've chosen the account type, the next step is to provide essential details about the account. Here's what you'll need to enter:

For Banking (Checking, Savings, or Cash) Accounts:

- **Account Name:** Give your account a clear and descriptive name (e.g., "Household Checking" or "Emergency Savings").

- **Account Type:** Confirm the type of account (checking, savings, or cash).

- **Starting Balance:** Enter the current balance of the account. For checking or savings accounts, you can refer to your most recent bank statement. For a cash account, this might be the amount of physical cash you have on hand.

For Loans:

- **Loan Name:** Name the loan for easy tracking (e.g., "Car Loan" or "Student Loan").

- **Loan Amount:** Enter the total amount of the loan or the current balance.

- **Interest Rate:** If you're tracking a loan, be sure to enter the interest rate so Quicken can help you calculate future payments.

- **Payment Schedule:** You can manually input the loan's payment schedule (monthly, quarterly, etc.).

For Investment Accounts:

- **Account Name:** Name the account according to its use (e.g., "Retirement IRA" or "Brokerage Account").
- **Investment Type:** Specify the type of investments held in the account, such as stocks, bonds, or mutual funds.
- **Initial Value:** Enter the starting value of the account. You can update this value over time by adding transactions or adjusting the account's performance manually.

Manually Adding Transactions

Once you've set up a manual account, it's important to regularly update the transactions to ensure the account reflects your financial activity. Here's how to add manual transactions:

Step 1

Go to the Account Register:

- Navigate to the account you just created by clicking on its name in the left panel.
- This will open the "Account Register", where you can view and manually input transactions.

Step 2

Enter Transactions:

- To add a new transaction, click "Add Transaction" at the top of the register.
- Manually input the date of the transaction, the payee, the category (e.g., "Groceries" or "Utilities"), and the amount.
- You can also add notes or tags to further categorize and track specific details.

Step 3

Split Transactions (if applicable):

If a single transaction involves multiple categories (for instance, if you purchased groceries, home goods, and personal care items in one trip), you can split the transaction into different categories. Click "Split" and assign amounts to each category.

Step 4

Adjust Balances Regularly:

For manually tracked accounts, it's important to update the balance regularly to ensure accuracy. For instance, with a cash account, you'll want to enter expenses as you spend money. Similarly, for loans, you can manually adjust the balance as you make payments.

Reconciling Manually Added Accounts

For accounts that are not linked to financial institutions, reconciling becomes a vital part of ensuring your financial records are accurate. Reconciling is the process of comparing your records in Quicken with your physical bank statements or loan documents to ensure everything matches.

Step 1

Obtain Your Latest Statement:

To reconcile an account, first get the most recent statement from your bank or lender. For cash accounts, you may reconcile against your own records or receipts.

Step 2

Reconcile in Quicken:

- In the account register, click "Reconcile" (this is typically found at the top of the account window).
- Enter the statement's ending balance and the date.
- Quicken will then display a list of transactions. Compare these with your statement and mark transactions as "cleared" if they match.
- If you notice any discrepancies, adjust the transactions accordingly. Once the balances match, you can finalize the reconciliation.

Step Three: Sorting Transactions

Categorizing your transactions in Quicken is one of the most important steps in managing your finances effectively. Proper categorization allows you to track where your money is going, set up budgets, and generate accurate reports that give you a clearer understanding of your financial health. Whether you are tracking income, expenses, or investments, assigning the correct category to each transaction ensures that your financial data is organized and easy to analyse. This step-by-step guide will walk you through the process of categorizing transactions in Quicken, explaining how to use categories, create custom ones, and make adjustments as needed.

Understanding the Importance of Categories

Categories are essential for organizing your financial transactions in Quicken. Each transaction you enter or download from your bank should be assigned to a specific category, such as "Groceries," "Rent," "Dining," or "Utilities." This allows you to group similar transactions together, making it easier to see how much you are spending in different areas of your life.

Proper categorization provides several benefits:

- Tracking Spending: You can easily see how much you're spending in specific areas, helping you manage your finances more effectively.

- Budgeting: Categorized transactions feed into your budget, allowing Quicken to compare your actual spending with your budgeted amounts.

- Tax Preparation: Categories like "Charitable Donations" or "Business Expenses" make tax time easier by helping you track deductible expenses.

- Financial Reports: Categorized transactions allow Quicken to generate detailed reports on your income, spending, and net worth.

Automatic Categorization in Quicken

When you link your bank accounts to Quicken, the software will automatically download transactions and attempt to assign categories based on the merchant or payee information. For example, if you make a payment to a supermarket, Quicken may automatically categorize it as "Groceries." This feature is helpful, but it's important to review the automatic categorizations, as they may not always be accurate.

Reviewing Automatically Categorized Transactions:

- Go to the Transaction Register: After Quicken downloads your recent transactions, navigate to the transaction register for the specific account by clicking on the account name in the left-hand panel.

- Check Each Category: Review the category assigned to each transaction. Automatic categories can sometimes be incorrect, especially if a merchant or payee could fit into multiple categories (e.g., a payment to a department store could be "Clothing" or "Household Supplies").

- Edit Categories: If a category is incorrect, simply click on the category field in the transaction and select a new one from the drop-down list.

Manually Categorizing Transactions

Step 1

Adding or Editing a Category:

- Select the Transaction: Click on the transaction you want to categorize in the register.

- Open the Category Field: Next to the transaction amount, you'll see a category field. Click on it to open the drop-down list of available categories.

- Choose a Category: Select the appropriate category from the list (e.g., "Dining," "Medical," "Utilities").

- Save the Transaction: Once you've selected the correct category, save the transaction by pressing Enter or clicking out of the field.

Step 2

Creating Custom Categories:

If the default categories in Quicken don't fit your specific financial situation, you can create custom categories to better organize your transactions. For example, you might want to create a custom category for "Pet Expenses" or "Online Subscriptions."

- Access the Category List: From the Quicken main menu, go to "Tools > Category List".

- Create a New Category: In the Category List window, click "New" to create a custom category. You'll be prompted to enter the category name and select whether it's an income or expense category.

- Assign a Parent Category (Optional): If your new category fits within a larger category, you can assign it as a subcategory. For example, you could create a "Streaming Services" subcategory under "Entertainment."

- Save the Category: Once you've entered all the necessary details, save the new category. It will now appear in the drop-down list whenever you categorize a transaction.

Step 3

Applying Custom Categories to Transactions:

Once your custom categories are set up, you can start assigning them to your transactions just like you would with Quicken's default categories. When categorizing a transaction, simply choose your custom category from the drop-down menu.

Splitting Transactions Across Multiple Categories

Some transactions may cover multiple expense categories, such as a trip to a store where you purchase groceries, clothing, and home supplies. In these cases, you can split the transaction in Quicken so that each part is categorized correctly.

Step 1

Selecting the Transaction:

Find the transaction in your register that needs to be split and click on it to open the details.

Step 2

Opening the Split Transaction Option:

Next to the category field, click on the "Split" button. This will open a window where you can divide the transaction into multiple parts.

Step 3

Assigning Categories and Amounts:

In the split transaction window, you can enter different amounts for each category. For example, if you spent $50 at a store and $30 was for groceries and $20 for household supplies, you would enter those amounts and select the appropriate categories.

Step 4

Saving the Split Transaction: After you've entered all the amounts and categories, click "OK" to save the split transaction. The transaction will now be divided in your register, and each portion will be reflected in the appropriate category.

CHAPTER FOUR: MAKING ACCOUNTS FOR YOUR EARNINGS AND EXPENDITURES

Understanding your financial landscape begins with a clear picture of your earnings and expenditures. Accounting for your earnings involves not just recording the money you bring in but also recognizing the various sources of income—whether it's your salary, freelance work, or investment returns. In this section, we'll explore practical strategies and tools, such as Quicken, that can simplify the process of tracking and analysing your financial activity. With the right approach, you'll gain valuable insights into your financial habits, enabling you to make better choices and ultimately leading to a more secure and prosperous financial future. Let's embark on this journey toward financial clarity and empowerment!

Using Quicken to Import Transactions

Importing transactions into Quicken is an essential process that allows you to keep your financial data up-to-date without manually entering every transaction. Whether you're downloading transactions directly from your bank or importing them from a file, Quicken makes it easy to ensure that all your financial activity is accurately reflected in the software. This guide will walk you through the steps to import transactions into Quicken, covering both automatic downloads from financial institutions and manual imports from files.

Bringing in Transactions from Financial Institutions

Quickens ability to connect directly with your bank, credit card, or investment account is one of its most convenient features. By linking your financial institution to Quicken, you can download transactions automatically, keeping your records up-to-date with minimal effort.

Step 1

Linking Your Bank Accounts

Before you can import transactions automatically, you need to link your bank accounts to Quicken. This process allows Quicken to download transactions directly from your financial institution. If you haven't already linked your accounts, follow these steps:

- **Go to the Add Account Section:** From the main dashboard or the left panel, select "Add Account".
- **Select Your Financial Institution:** Choose the type of account you want to link (e.g., Checking, Savings, or Credit Card) and search for your bank or financial institution from the list provided.
- **Log In to Your Bank:** Enter your online banking credentials to allow Quicken to securely connect to your account. You may need to complete two-factor authentication depending on your bank's security settings.
- **Select Accounts:** Choose which accounts you want to link to Quicken and confirm the connection.

Once your accounts are linked, Quicken will begin downloading transactions directly from your bank.

Step 2

Downloading Transactions

After linking your accounts, Quicken will automatically download transactions every time you update the account. To manually trigger a download of recent transactions, follow these steps:

- **Select the Account:** Go to the account you wish to update by clicking on it in the left panel.

- **Click Update:** At the top of the transaction register, you'll see an "Update" button. Clicking this will download all recent transactions from your financial institution.

- **Review Transactions:** Once the download is complete, Quicken will display the imported transactions in your account register. These transactions are automatically categorized based on merchant or payee information, but you should review them to ensure accuracy.

Manually Importing Transactions from a File

If your bank doesn't support automatic syncing with Quicken or you prefer to import transactions manually, you can upload them using a compatible file format. Most financial institutions allow you to download transaction histories in formats that Quicken can import, such as QFX (Quicken Financial Exchange), QIF (Quicken Interchange Format), or CSV (Comma-Separated Values).

Step 1:

Downloading the Transaction File from Your Bank

First, you'll need to download a file containing your transaction history from your bank's website.

1. **Log In to Your Bank:** Visit your bank's website and log in to your account.

2. **Find the Export/Download Option:** Navigate to the section of your account where you can view or download your transaction history. This is usually under a menu labelled "Statements" or "Transaction History."

3. **Choose a Date Range:** Select the time period for which you want to download transactions (e.g., the last 30 days or a custom date range).

4. **Choose a File Format:** Select the file format that is compatible with Quicken. The most common formats are:

   - QFX (Web Connect): This is Quickens preferred file format and is compatible with both Windows and Mac versions of the software.

   - QIF: Older file format, still used for certain types of accounts or financial institutions.

   - CSV: A common format that may require some additional formatting in Quicken after importing.

5. **Download the File:** Save the file to a location on your computer that is easy to find, such as your Downloads folder.

Step 2:

Importing the File into Quicken

Once you've downloaded the file from your bank, the next step is to import it into Quicken. The process may vary slightly depending on the file format you're using, but the general steps are as follows:

1. **Go to File > Import:** Open Quicken and navigate to the "File" menu. Select "Import" from the dropdown menu.

2. **Select the File Format:** Choose the file format that matches the one you downloaded from your bank (e.g., QFX, QIF, or CSV).

3. **Locate the File:** Browse to the location where you saved the transaction file and select it for import.

4. **Match the Account:** Quicken will ask you to match the transactions to one of your existing accounts or create a new account if necessary. Select the appropriate account from the list.

5. **Review and Confirm:** Quicken will show a preview of the transactions being imported. Review the transactions to ensure they are correct, then click "OK" or "Import" to complete the process.

Step 3:

Categorizing and Reviewing Imported Transactions

After the import is complete, Quicken will automatically categorize the transactions based on the information provided by your bank. However, it's important to review the imported transactions to ensure they are assigned to the correct categories. Here's how:

1. **Go to the Account Register:** Navigate to the account where the transactions were imported.

2. **Review Categories:** Check each transaction to make sure it is categorized correctly. If necessary, manually change the categories by clicking on the category field and selecting the appropriate one from the drop-down menu.

3. **Add Notes or Tags:** If you want to add additional information for easier tracking, such as notes or tags, you can do so at this point.

4. **Save the Changes:** After reviewing and adjusting any categories or information, save your changes.

Configuring Repeating Transactions in Quicken

Setting up recurring transactions in Quicken is a key step to automating your financial management. Whether it's monthly bills, regular income, or recurring subscriptions, Quicken allows you to schedule these transactions to automatically appear in your account registers. This feature helps you stay on top of your financial commitments, avoid missing payments, and ensure that your cash flow is accurately tracked. Below is a step-by-step guide to setting up and managing recurring transactions in Quicken.

Understanding Recurring Transactions

A recurring transaction is any transaction that repeats on a regular basis, such as:

- Income: Regular payments like a monthly salary or rental income.
- Bills: Recurring expenses like utility bills, loan payments, rent, or insurance premiums.
- Subscriptions: Monthly or annual services like streaming platforms, gym memberships, or software subscriptions.
- Investments: Regular transfers to investment accounts or retirement savings.

By setting these up in Quicken, you automate the process of logging these transactions, making your financial management more efficient and accurate.

Adding a Recurring Transaction

To add a recurring transaction in Quicken, follow these steps:

Step 1:

Navigate to the Bill and Income Reminders Section

- **From the Main Dashboard:** On the main dashboard, find the "Bills & Income" tab at the top of the screen or in the left navigation panel.

- **Click on Manage Bill and Income Reminders:** Under this section, click on "Manage Bill and Income Reminders". This will bring up a window where you can manage existing reminders or add new ones.

Step 2:

Adding a New Recurring Transaction

- **Click on Add Reminder:** In the Bill and Income Reminders section, you'll see an option to "Add Reminder". Click this to add a new recurring transaction.

- **Select the Type of Reminder:** Quicken will prompt you to choose between a "Bill Reminder" or "Income Reminder" depending on whether the transaction is an expense or income. Choose the one that fits your needs.

Step 3:

Enter Transaction Details

Next, you'll need to enter details for the recurring transaction:

- **Payee or Source:** Enter the name of the payee (for bills) or source (for income), such as "Electric Company," "Mortgage Payment," or "Salary."

- **Amount:** Enter the exact amount of the recurring transaction. For variable amounts (like utilities that fluctuate monthly), you can leave this field blank or enter an estimated amount.

- **Category:** Select the appropriate category for the transaction. For example, "Utilities" for an electricity bill or "Salary" for regular income.

- **Frequency:** Choose how often the transaction repeats—monthly, weekly, bi-weekly, annually, or another custom schedule.

- **Start Date:** Set the date when the recurring transaction should begin. This could be the next payment or the upcoming payday.

- **End Date (Optional):** If the recurring transaction is only temporary (e.g., a loan payment that ends after a certain period), you can set an end date for the transaction.

Step 4:

Confirm and Save

Once you've entered all the relevant details, click "OK" or "Save" to finalize the recurring transaction. It will now appear in your account register based on the frequency you specified.

Managing and Editing Recurring Transactions

Over time, you may need to adjust or delete recurring transactions if amounts change or if payments end. Here's how to manage your recurring transactions in Quicken:

Step 1:

Viewing Existing Recurring Transactions

- **Go to the Bills & Income Section:** Open the "Bills & Income" tab from the dashboard or the left-hand panel.

- **View Your List of Reminders:** In the Bill and Income Reminders window, you'll see a list of all your recurring transactions, along with their next scheduled date and amount.

Step 2:

Editing a Recurring Transaction

- **Select the Transaction:** Click on the transaction you want to modify. This will open the reminder's details.
- **Make Adjustments:** You can change the payee, amount, category, frequency, or any other detail. For example, if your rent increases or your salary changes, simply update the amount in the transaction details.
- **Save Changes:** Once you've made the necessary adjustments, click "Save" to apply the changes.

Step 3:

Deleting or Ending a Recurring Transaction

If a recurring transaction is no longer necessary, such as a loan that's been paid off or a cancelled subscription, you can remove it from Quicken.

- **Select the Transaction:** In the Bill and Income Reminders window, click on the transaction you want to delete.
- **Delete or End the Transaction:** Depending on your version of Quicken, you'll either see an option to "Delete" the transaction or to "End Reminder".
- **Delete:** Removes the transaction entirely from Quicken, including any future scheduled occurrences.
- **End Reminder:** Stops the transaction from continuing in the future while preserving the history of past payments.

Using Recurring Transactions for Budgeting and Forecasting

One of the biggest advantages of setting up recurring transactions in Quicken is how it helps with budgeting and forecasting. Recurring transactions are automatically factored into your budget, ensuring that your income and expenses are accounted for. Additionally, recurring transactions provide valuable insights into your future cash flow.

Step 1:

Viewing Future Transactions

- **Go to the Bills & Income Section:** Open the Bills & Income tab to view both upcoming bills and income.
- **View Upcoming Payments and Deposits:** This section will display all scheduled transactions for the next several months, allowing you to plan accordingly.

Step 2:

Monitoring Cash Flow

- **Cash Flow Forecast:** By setting up all recurring income and expenses, quickens cash flow forecast feature can project your future account balances. This helps you anticipate when funds may be tight and adjust your spending or savings accordingly.
- **Adjusting Budgets:** Quicken will automatically integrate recurring transactions into your budget, making it easy to see how they affect your overall financial goals.

Using Tags and Notes in Quicken

Using tags and notes in Quicken is a powerful way to add another layer of organization and detail to your financial transactions. Tags allow you to group related transactions across multiple categories or accounts, while notes let you add detailed explanations or reminders for individual transactions. Together, these features make it easier to track specific spending patterns, monitor expenses related to particular events or projects, and improve your overall financial record-keeping. This step-by-step guide will help you understand how to use tags and notes effectively in Quicken.

Understanding the Purpose of Tags and Notes

Tags and notes serve different but complementary purposes in Quicken:

- Tags: Tags are labels you can assign to transactions to group them across various categories and accounts. Unlike categories, which are fixed for specific types of income or expenses, tags allow you to track related expenses that might span multiple categories. For example, you might use tags for "Vacation," "Work Project," or "Home Renovation" to track all expenses related to those events, regardless of which category (e.g., travel, dining, or supplies) they fall under.

- Notes: Notes are brief explanations or additional information you can attach to a transaction. They help provide context for the transaction, making it easier to remember why the expense was made or any important details associated with it. For instance, you could add a note to a business dinner transaction, explaining who attended and the purpose of the meeting.

Adding Tags to Transactions

Tags in Quicken allow you to group transactions related to specific events, projects, or activities, regardless of their category. This gives you a broader perspective on your spending habits or income sources tied to particular goals.

Step 1:

Navigating to the Transaction Register

- Open the Account Register: From the left-hand panel, select the account where the transaction is recorded. This will open the transaction register, where you can view and edit individual transactions.

- Locate the Transaction: Scroll through the transaction list to find the one to which you want to add a tag.

Step 2:

Adding or Editing Tags

- Click on the Transaction: Select the transaction you want to tag by clicking on it.

- Find the Tag Field: To the right of the transaction's category field, you'll see a "Tags" field.

- Add a Tag: Click into the tag field and type the name of the tag you want to use. If you've previously created tags, a drop-down menu will appear, allowing you to select from existing tags. If it's a new tag, just type the name and press Enter.

- Save the Transaction: Once you've added the tag, press Enter or click outside the field to save the transaction with the new tag attached.

Step 3:

Using Multiple Tags

You can assign more than one tag to a single transaction, which is helpful when a transaction falls under multiple projects or events. For example, if you're tracking both "Vacation" and "Summer 2024," you can apply both tags to a travel-related transaction by separating them with a comma.

Managing and Customizing Tags

As you start using tags, it's important to manage and organize them for easy tracking. Quicken allows you to create, edit, and delete tags as needed.

Step 1:

Viewing Your Tags

- Open the Tag List: To manage your tags, go to Tools > Tag List in the main menu. This will display all the tags you've created or used across your transactions.

- Review Tags: Here, you can see which tags are in use and how frequently they're applied to your transactions.

Step 2:

Creating Custom Tags

- Create a New Tag: From the Tag List window, click New Tag to create a new custom tag.

- Define the Tag: Enter a name for the tag and a description (optional). You can use tags for anything that is relevant to your financial management—such as "House Repairs," "Business Expenses," or "Holiday Shopping."

- Save the Tag: Once you've named your new tag, click OK to save it. It will now be available for use in future transactions.

Step 3:

Deleting or Renaming Tags

- Edit or Delete a Tag: In the Tag List, you can also choose to delete tags you no longer need or rename existing tags for better clarity. Simply select the tag you wish to modify, then click "Edit" or "Delete" from the options.

- Merge Tags: If you've accidentally created duplicate tags or want to combine tags that serve the same purpose, you can merge them by selecting both tags and clicking "Merge".

Adding Notes to Transactions

Notes in Quicken provide valuable context or additional information about a transaction. This can be particularly useful for clarifying the reason behind a payment or tracking specific details like reimbursement claims or business expenses.

Step 1:

Adding Notes to a Transaction

- Select the Transaction: Find the transaction you want to add a note to in the account register.

- Open the Notes Field: In most versions of Quicken, the notes field is located in the transaction details, either as a dedicated column or within the expanded details of the transaction.

- Enter the Note: Click on the note field and type in the information you want to include. For example, if you're adding a note to a business expense, you might write, "Dinner with client, discussed upcoming project."

- Save the Transaction: After entering your note, press Enter or click outside the field to save it.

Step 2:

Viewing and Editing Notes

- View Notes: You can view the notes associated with any transaction by opening the transaction register and expanding the details of a specific transaction. Notes are typically displayed as an icon or text field next to the transaction amount or category.

- Edit Notes: To edit a note, click on the note field, make the necessary changes, and save the transaction.

Using Tags and Notes in Reports

One of the most powerful ways to leverage tags and notes in Quicken is through the reporting feature. By including tags and notes in your reports, you can gain deeper insights into specific areas of your finances.

Step 1:

Generating Reports with Tags

- Go to Reports: In Quicken, go to the "Reports" tab and select the type of report you want to generate, such as "Spending by Category" or "Income vs. Expenses".

- Filter by Tag: When setting the report parameters, you can filter transactions by tags. For example, you could generate a report that only shows transactions tagged with "Vacation" to track how much you've spent on your trip.

- Review the Report: The report will display only the transactions associated with the selected tag, giving you a clear view of how much you've spent or earned related to that tag.

Step 2:

Using Notes for Reference

While Quicken does not directly include notes in standard reports, you can still use them for reference when reviewing transactions. As you go through your account registers or reports, you can expand the transaction details to view the notes you've added. This can be especially useful when preparing for taxes or reviewing expenses for reimbursement.

Using tags and notes in Quicken gives you greater flexibility and control over your financial data. Tags allow you to track transactions across different categories and accounts, making it easier to monitor specific events or projects. Notes add an extra layer of detail, ensuring that you can keep track of important information related to individual transactions. By integrating tags and notes into your financial management, you can improve the accuracy and organization of your records while gaining valuable insights into your spending and income patterns.

CHAPTER FIVE: BUGDGET MANAGEMENT USING QUICKEN

Budgeting can often feel like a chore, but with Quicken, it becomes an empowering tool to achieve your financial goals and build a more secure future. Quickens budget management features allow you to take control of your finances by creating a clear, personalized plan that's easy to set up and maintain. With Quicken, you can track your income, categorize expenses, and set spending limits in a way that fits your unique lifestyle. By having all your finances in one place, you'll gain a real-time overview of where your money is going and how to stay on track. Whether you're saving for a vacation, paying down debt, or planning for major life events, Quickens budget management tools make it simple to stay organized, avoid overspending, and make smarter financial choices. In this section, we'll dive into the essential steps to create, customize, and manage your budget with Quicken. Let's get started on building a budget that works for you!

Making a Budget with Quicken

Creating a budget is one of the most effective ways to take control of your finances. Quicken provides a simple, intuitive budgeting tool that helps you set financial goals, track your income and expenses, and monitor your progress over time. Whether you're saving for a big purchase, trying to reduce debt, or just want to ensure you're living within your means, a budget in Quicken can provide the structure you need. This guide will walk you through the steps to create a budget in Quicken and customize it to fit your financial needs.

Understanding Why a Budget is Important

A budget is a financial plan that outlines your income and spending, helping you stay on track to meet your financial goals. By setting up a budget in Quicken, you'll be able to:

- Monitor Spending: See exactly where your money is going and identify areas where you may be overspending.

- Plan for Savings: Allocate part of your income to savings for short-term and long-term goals.

- Avoid Debt: Ensure you're living within your means by comparing your expenses to your income.

- Track Progress: Quicken allows you to track your progress against your budget, showing you how much you've spent in each category relative to your planned spending.

Setting Up Your Budget in Quicken

Before you begin creating a budget, make sure all your financial accounts (checking, savings, credit cards, etc.) are linked to Quicken so that your transactions are automatically imported and categorized. Once your accounts are set up, follow these steps to create a budget.

Step 1:

Navigating to the Budgeting Section

- Go to the Planning Tab: Open Quicken and navigate to the "Planning" tab from the main toolbar. This is where you'll find the budgeting tools.
- Click on Create New Budget: In the Planning tab, select "Create New Budget" to start setting up your personalized budget.

Step 2:

Choosing the Budget Year

- Select a Time Frame: Quicken will prompt you to choose the year for your budget. Most people create budgets on an annual basis, but you can also set up budgets for a specific period, such as a quarter or month, depending on your financial planning needs.
- Click Next: After selecting the budget year or time frame, click "Next" to proceed.

Adding Income to Your Budget

Your budget should start by accounting for all sources of income. This ensures you have an accurate picture of how much money you're working with.

Step 1:

Entering Income Categories

- Add Income Sources: In the budgeting tool, you'll see a list of categories for income. These are typically categorized as salary, bonuses, freelance work, or other sources. If your income comes from multiple sources, be sure to list each one individually.

- Estimate Income Amounts: Enter an estimated monthly income for each source. If your income varies from month to month, it's a good idea to use an average based on past months or set conservative estimates to avoid overestimating your available funds.

Step 2:

Adding Custom Income Categories

- Create New Categories: If Quickens default categories don't fit your specific income streams, you can create custom categories. For example, if you receive rental income or income from side jobs, create custom categories by clicking "Add Category".
- Enter Expected Income: Once you've added the custom income category, input your estimated earnings for each month.

Adding Expenses to Your Budget

Next, it's time to account for all your regular expenses, which may include fixed expenses like rent or mortgage payments as well as variable expenses like groceries, entertainment, and utilities.

Step 1:

Categorizing Expenses

- Review Expense Categories: Quicken automatically provides a list of common expense categories, such as rent, utilities, groceries, and transportation. Review this list to ensure it matches your regular spending.

- Add Custom Expense Categories: If you have specific expenses that don't fit into Quickens pre-set categories, you can create custom expense categories. For example, if you have recurring expenses for hobbies, childcare, or health-related costs, you can create categories for each.
- Set Monthly Limits: For each category, input the maximum amount you plan to spend each month. Be realistic and use past spending data (which Quicken tracks) to help set appropriate limits.

Step 2:

Planning for Variable Expenses

- Enter Estimates for Variable Costs: Some expenses fluctuate month to month, like utility bills, dining out, or transportation costs. Estimate your average monthly spending based on historical data or anticipated future spending.
- Adjust Over Time: As you begin to track your budget, adjust the estimates for variable expenses as necessary. Quicken makes it easy to tweak your budget to reflect real-world spending.

Setting Financial Goals

An effective budget isn't just about limiting spending—it's also a tool to help you achieve financial goals, such as saving for a vacation, paying off debt, or building an emergency fund.

Step 1:

Adding Savings Goals

- Create Savings Categories: Add categories for each of your savings' goals. For example, you might have categories like "Emergency Fund," "Vacation Savings," or "Home Improvement Fund."

- Set Target Amounts: For each savings goal, set a target amount and decide how much you want to contribute each month. Quicken will track your progress toward each goal, showing you how close you are to reaching your target.

Step 2:

Allocating Funds to Debt Payments

- Include Debt Payments: If you're working to pay off debt, add categories for debt payments, such as credit card payments, student loans, or auto loans.

- Set Payment Amounts: Enter your planned monthly payments and, if possible, allocate extra funds to pay down debt faster. Quicken will help you track how much progress you're making on reducing your balances over time.

Reviewing and Adjusting Your Budget

Once your budget is set up with income, expenses, savings, and debt payments, it's important to review it regularly and make adjustments as needed. Quicken makes it easy to monitor your budget performance and adjust spending categories if your financial situation changes.

Step 1:

Tracking Your Progress

- View the Budget Summary: In the Planning tab, Quicken will show you a summary of your budget, including a comparison of your planned spending vs. actual spending for each category.

- Track Monthly Trends: Quicken allows you to track your spending trends over time. If you consistently overspend in one category, you can adjust your budget to account for it.

Step 2:

Making Adjustments

- Edit Budget Categories: If you find that your initial estimates for income or expenses are off, you can easily adjust your budget categories by clicking on the category and modifying the amount.

- Reallocate Funds: If you're underspending in one category and overspending in another, Quicken lets you reallocate funds to make sure your overall budget stays balanced.

1. **Using Quicken's Budget Alerts and Reports**

Quicken's budget feature offers alerts and reports to help you stay on track and monitor your financial performance.

Step 1:

Setting Up Budget Alerts

- Enable Alerts: Quicken allows you to set up alerts that notify you when you're close to reaching your spending limit in a particular category or when you've gone over your budget.

- Customize Notifications: You can choose to receive these alerts via email or directly in the app, ensuring you stay aware of your financial status in real time.

Step 2:

Generating Budget Reports

- Generate Monthly or Annual Reports: Quicken can create detailed budget reports showing your spending habits over time. These reports help you analyse how well you've stuck to your budget and where you can make improvements.
- Use Reports for Better Financial Decisions: By reviewing these reports regularly, you can make more informed financial decisions, identify trends, and adjust your spending habits as needed.

Creating a budget in Quicken is an excellent way to take control of your finances and work toward your financial goals. By setting up income, expenses, and savings categories, you can track your financial activity in real-time and adjust your budget as your situation changes. Quickens budgeting tools provide valuable insights into your spending patterns and help you stay on track with both short- and long-term financial goals. With regular monitoring and adjustments, your Quicken budget will become an essential tool in your financial success.

Tracking Spending Against Your Budget in Quicken

Tracking your spending is one of the most important steps in managing your budget effectively. Quicken makes this process simple by automatically tracking and categorizing your expenses so you can see how well you're sticking to your budget.

Monitoring your spending against your planned budget in real-time gives you the ability to make informed decisions, adjust spending habits, and avoid overspending in various categories. This step-by-step guide will show you how to track your spending in Quicken and ensure that you're staying on top of your budget.

How Quicken Tracks Your Spending

Once you've set up your budget categories in Quicken, the software will automatically track your spending by importing transactions from your linked financial accounts. Quicken uses the categories you've assigned to your budget to categorize each transaction, showing you how much you've spent in each area. If you enter transactions manually, you can also categorize these expenses to ensure they're properly accounted for in your budget.

Automatic Categorization of Transactions

- Linked Accounts: For accounts linked to Quicken (such as checking, savings, and credit cards), your transactions will automatically download and be categorized based on the payee or merchant. For instance, if you purchase groceries, Quicken will assign the transaction to the "Groceries" category.
- Manual Transactions: If you're entering transactions manually, simply assign the appropriate category when you input the transaction. You can also split transactions into multiple categories if they cover different types of expenses (for example, groceries and household items in the same transaction).

Viewing Your Spending vs. Budget

Quicken provides a visual overview of your spending in relation to your budget, making it easy to see how much you've spent in each category and whether you're within your limits.

Step 1:

Accessing the Budget Overview

- Go to the Planning Tab: From the main toolbar, click on the "Planning" tab. This will open the budgeting section of Quicken, where you can view your budget categories and see how your spending compares to your plan.

- View Spending by Category: The budget overview displays your spending for each category compared to your budgeted amount. Categories where you are under budget will show in green, while categories where you've overspent will appear in red or with a warning icon.

Step 2:

Reviewing Your Spending Progress

- Track Monthly Spending: Quicken allows you to track your spending on a monthly basis, making it easy to see how your spending habits align with your budget for the current month. The software provides a bar graph or pie chart that visually represents your spending vs. budgeted amounts for each category.

- Check Remaining Budget: Each category in the budget overview shows the amount you've spent, the budgeted amount, and the remaining balance. This makes it clear how much you have left to spend in each category before hitting your budget limit.

Adjusting Spending as Needed

Tracking your spending in real-time allows you to make adjustments if you're close to overspending in any category. By keeping an eye on your budget throughout the month, you can make small changes to stay within your limits.

Step 1:

Adjusting Spending Within Categories

- Reallocating Funds: If you notice that you're approaching the limit in one category but underspending in another, Quicken allows you to adjust your budget. You can reallocate funds from categories where you're under budget to cover areas where you might overspend. **Example:** If you're under budget in "Dining Out" but over budget in "Groceries," you can adjust your grocery budget by moving some of the excess funds from the dining category.

- Reducing Spending in Certain Areas: If reallocating funds isn't an option, tracking your budget early allows you to adjust your spending behaviour. For instance, if you're overspending in entertainment or shopping, you can decide to cut back on these expenses for the remainder of the month.

Step 2:

Setting Alerts for Overspending

- Enabling Budget Alerts: Quicken offers alerts that notify you when you're close to reaching your budgeted amount in a particular category. You can enable alerts for individual categories so that you're reminded when your spending is nearing the limit.

- Customizing Alerts: You can customize how and when Quicken sends alerts. These notifications can be sent directly to your email or appear within the software, helping you stay informed and in control of your budget.

Analysing Spending Patterns

Quickens reporting tools allow you to analyse your spending habits over time, providing insights into areas where you might be consistently overspending or underspending. Understanding these patterns can help you fine-tune your budget and make more informed financial decisions.

Step 1:

Generating Spending Reports

- Go to Reports Tab: In Quickens main menu, click on the "Reports" tab, where you can generate various financial reports, including a "Spending by Category" report.
- Select Time Frame: Choose the time frame for the report (monthly, quarterly, or annually) to see how your spending compares to your budget over time.
- View Spending Trends: The report will show you how much you've spent in each category and how that spending has changed over time. This can help you identify patterns or habits, such as consistently overspending in certain categories.

Step 2:

Identifying Areas for Improvement

- Review Categories with Frequent Overspending: Use Quicken's reports to identify categories where you're frequently overspending. If you notice that certain expenses, such as dining out or entertainment, are consistently over budget, consider adjusting your spending habits in those areas.
- Make Adjustments to Budget: Based on the insights from your spending report, you can make adjustments to your budget. For example, if you're

consistently spending more on groceries than expected, you may need to increase your grocery budget while cutting back in another area.

Staying On Track with Long-Term Goals

One of the key benefits of tracking your spending in Quicken is that it helps you stay focused on your long-term financial goals, such as saving for a house, paying off debt, or building an emergency fund.

Step 1:

Allocating Funds to Savings

- Review Your Savings Goals: Quicken allows you to set up and track savings goals, such as building an emergency fund or saving for a vacation. By regularly reviewing your spending, you can ensure that you're allocating enough funds to meet these goals.

- Adjust Spending to Prioritize Savings: If you're underspending in certain areas, consider redirecting those funds toward your savings goals. Quicken's budgeting tools allow you to make these adjustments easily to ensure you're staying on track.

Step 2:

Monitoring Cash Flow

- Review Your Cash Flow: Quickens cash flow feature shows how your income compares to your expenses each month. By keeping a close eye on cash flow, you can avoid running into financial trouble and ensure that you're living within your means.

- Avoiding Debt: Regularly tracking your spending helps you avoid overspending and accumulating unnecessary debt. By staying on top of your budget, you can keep your finances in check and ensure you're working toward financial stability.

Tracking your spending against your budget in Quicken is crucial to maintaining financial control and staying on track with your financial goals. Quicken provides powerful tools to monitor spending in real-time, adjust your budget as needed, and analyze spending patterns to help you make smarter financial decisions. By regularly reviewing your spending and making proactive adjustments, you can avoid overspending, prioritize savings, and ensure that your budget remains balanced. With Quicken's alerts, reports, and customization features, you can easily stay on top of your finances and work toward long-term financial success.

Setting Alerts and Notifications in Quicken

One of the most powerful features of Quicken is its ability to send alerts and notifications to help you stay on top of your financial situation. Whether you're managing your budget, monitoring your bank balances, or tracking bill payments, setting up alerts ensures you remain informed about important financial activities. Alerts and notifications can help you avoid overspending, prevent missed payments, and manage cash flow more effectively. This guide will walk you through the steps to set up alerts and notifications in Quicken.

Why Use Alerts and Notifications?

Alerts and notifications in Quicken serve as real-time reminders and updates that help you manage your finances with ease. Here are a few reasons why they're essential:

- Prevent Overspending: Alerts notify you when you're approaching or exceeding your budget limits in specific categories.
- Avoid Late Payments: Receive reminders for upcoming bill payments to avoid missing due dates and incurring late fees.
- Monitor Account Balances: Stay informed about your account balances so you can prevent overdrafts and manage your cash flow.
- Track Income: Get notifications when expected income, such as a salary or rental income, is deposited into your account.

By setting up custom alerts, you can tailor notifications to meet your personal financial needs, helping you stay organized and proactive about managing your money.

Accessing the Alerts and Notifications Settings

Before setting up specific alerts, you first need to access the alerts and notifications section in Quicken. Follow these steps to get started:

Step 1:

Navigating to the Alerts Center

- Open Quicken: Launch the Quicken software on your computer.
- Go to Tools Menu: From the main Quicken dashboard, click on the "Tools" menu at the top of the screen.

- Select Alerts Centre: From the drop-down menu, select "Alerts Centre". This will open a window where you can manage your alerts and notifications.

Step 2:

Exploring the Alerts Centre

Once you're in the Alerts Centre, you'll see a list of different types of alerts that Quicken offers. These include:

- Spending Alerts: For monitoring spending in budget categories.
- Bill and Income Alerts: For keeping track of upcoming bill payments and expected income.
- Account Balance Alerts: For monitoring account balances and preventing overdrafts.
- Investment Alerts: For tracking changes in your investment portfolio.

You can customize these alerts based on your preferences and financial goals.

Setting Up Spending Alerts

Spending alerts help you track your expenses and ensure you're staying within your budget. You can set up spending alerts to notify you when you're nearing or exceeding your budgeted amount for specific categories.

Step 1:

Enabling Spending Alerts

- Go to Spending Alerts: In the Alerts Center, find the section labelled "Spending Alerts".

- Select Budget Categories: Choose the budget categories you want to monitor, such as "Groceries," "Entertainment," or "Utilities."

- Set Spending Thresholds: Specify a threshold for each category. For example, you can set an alert to notify you when you've spent 80% of your grocery budget for the month. You can also set a second alert to notify you when you've exceeded your total budget in that category.

Step 2:

Customizing Spending Alerts

- Frequency of Alerts: Choose how frequently you want to receive alerts. You can receive them daily, weekly, or only when certain spending thresholds are met.

- Delivery Method: Choose how you want to be notified—either through in-app notifications, email, or both. Quicken makes it easy to customize notifications based on how often you want to be updated.

Setting Up Bill and Income Alerts

Bill and income alerts are crucial for staying on top of payments and incoming funds. These alerts ensure you never miss a payment or forget to record an expected deposit.

Step 1:

Enabling Bill Payment Alerts

- Go to Bill Alerts: In the Alerts Center, navigate to the "Bill and Income Alerts" section.

- Set Up Bill Reminders: For each bill you want to monitor, select the reminder option. You can choose to receive alerts before a bill is due—typically a few days before the due date.

- Configure Late Payment Alerts: You can also set up an alert to notify you if a bill is overdue, helping you avoid late fees.

Step 2:

Enabling Income Alert

- Track Expected Income: In the "Bill and Income Alerts" section, you can also set up alerts for income. For example, if you receive a paycheck or rental income on a regular basis, you can configure an alert to notify you when the income is deposited into your account.

- Set Alerts for Missed Deposits: You can configure Quicken to notify you if expected income isn't deposited by a certain date, which is helpful for managing irregular or delayed payments.

Setting Up Account Balance Alerts

Account balance alerts are useful for keeping an eye on your bank account balances and ensuring you have enough funds to cover expenses. These alerts can help you avoid overdrafts or ensure that your savings account reaches a certain balance.

Step 1:

Enabling Balance Alerts

- Go to Account Balance Alerts: In the Alerts Center, find the section for "Account Balance Alerts".

- Set Minimum Balance Thresholds: You can set alerts to notify you when your checking or savings account balance falls below a certain amount. For example, you might want an alert when your checking account balance drops below $500 to ensure you don't overdraw your account.

- Set Maximum Balance Thresholds: You can also set alerts for when your account reaches a certain balance. For example, if you're saving for a goal, you can get notified when your savings account reaches a target amount.

Step 2:

Monitoring Cash Flow

- Monitor Daily Balances: Quicken can also send you daily notifications about your account balances, allowing you to keep track of your cash flow. This feature is especially useful if you want to stay up-to-date on your financial situation without logging into Quicken every day.

- Configure Overdraft Alerts: If you're worried about overdrawing your account, you can set an alert to notify you when your balance is dangerously low, helping you take action before an overdraft occurs.

Setting Up Investment Alerts

If you have investment accounts linked to Quicken, setting up investment alerts can help you monitor changes in your portfolio and stay informed about market activity.

Step 1:

Enabling Investment Alerts

- Go to Investment Alerts: In the Alerts Center, navigate to the "Investment Alerts" section.

- Set Alerts for Market Changes: Quicken allows you to set up alerts for changes in the value of your investments. For example, you can set an alert to notify you when a stock in your portfolio increases or decreases by a certain percentage.

- Track Dividends and Interest: You can also set alerts to notify you when you receive dividends or interest payments from your investments.

Step 2:

Monitoring Portfolio Performance

- Track Portfolio Value: Set up an alert to notify you when the total value of your investment portfolio changes significantly, helping you stay informed about the overall performance of your investments.

- Configure Gain/Loss Alerts: If you're tracking specific securities, Quicken can send alerts when a stock reaches a certain gain or loss threshold, allowing you to make informed decisions about buying or selling.

Managing and Customizing Alerts

Once your alerts and notifications are set up, it's important to manage and adjust them based on your changing financial needs.

Step 1:

Reviewing Active Alerts

- Check Active Alerts: In the Alerts Centre, you can view a list of all active alerts. This allows you to see what notifications are currently enabled and make adjustments as necessary.

- Edit Alerts: If your spending habits, income, or bill schedules change, you can easily edit existing alerts by selecting the alert and modifying the parameters.

Step 2:

Turning Off or Deleting Alerts

- Disable Alerts: If you no longer need a particular alert, you can disable it by unchecking the box next to the alert in the Alerts Centre.

- Delete Alerts: To remove an alert permanently, select the alert and click" Delete". This will stop the notification from appearing in the future.

Setting up alerts and notifications in Quicken is a powerful way to stay on top of your finances. Whether you're tracking spending, managing bills, monitoring account balances, or keeping an eye on your investments, these alerts ensure you're always informed about your financial activity. By customizing alerts to your specific needs, you can avoid overspending, prevent missed payments, and stay on track with your financial goals. With Quickens flexible alert system, you'll have the tools you need to manage your money effectively and make proactive decisions about your finances.

CHAPTER SIX: MANAGING BILLS AND INCOME WITH REMINDERS

Balancing multiple bills and tracking various income sources can easily become overwhelming in today's busy world. Whether it's a mortgage payment, utilities, credit card bills, or different pay checks, staying on top of your finances requires organization and consistency. This is where quickens powerful bill and income management features come into play, helping you take control of your cash flow with ease and confidence. In this chapter, we'll explore how Quickens tools can help you effectively manage all aspects of your monthly finances, from tracking each income source to setting up reminders for every bill due date. With Quickens automated bill reminders, you'll never miss a payment or risk late fees again. By setting up clear reminders and organizing your cash flow, you'll reduce stress and gain a clearer picture of your financial landscape. Let's dive into how you can use Quicken to make managing bills and income straightforward and stress-free, giving you peace of mind and the freedom to focus on your bigger financial goals.

Managing Bills and Income

Effectively managing bills and income is a cornerstone of financial stability, and Quicken offers tools to help you stay organized, avoid missed payments, and make the most of your cash flow. By setting up bill tracking and income logging in Quicken, you can see exactly where your money is going and when it's coming in—making it easier to plan, budget, and reduce financial stress.

1. Organizing Your Bills

Quicken allows you to list all your recurring bills, from utilities and rent to loan payments and credit card bills. By adding each bill along with its due date, amount, and payment frequency, you create a complete overview of your monthly obligations. Quickens dashboard will show upcoming bills, helping you plan your cash flow and avoid surprises.

2. Setting Up Reminders

With Quickens reminders feature, you can schedule alerts for each bill. Set them to notify you days or weeks before the due date, so you're always ahead of schedule. Automatic reminders not only prevent late fees but also allow you to plan payments based on your income schedule, ensuring you have sufficient funds when each bill is due.

3. Tracking Income Sources

Whether you have a single pay check or multiple income streams, Quicken helps you track each source individually. From salaries to freelance payments or investments, logging income ensures you know exactly how much money is coming in and from where. With this feature, you can monitor fluctuations in income and adjust your budgeting as needed.

4. Creating a Balanced Cash Flow

Once your bills and income are entered into Quicken, the software helps you create a balanced cash flow by comparing upcoming expenses against expected income. Quickens forecasting tools offer a glimpse into your financial future, showing any potential shortfalls or surplus cash, you can save or reinvest. This comprehensive view enables you to make adjustments and optimize your financial health.

5. Reviewing and Adjusting Regularly

Quicken makes it easy to review your financial data over time. Regularly checking your income and bill history helps you spot trends, adjust budgets, and plan for any upcoming changes, such as new bills or variable income. By staying proactive, you ensure your finances are always aligned with your goals.

Managing bills and income becomes far less overwhelming with Quickens intuitive tools. With a structured system in place, you can confidently stay on top of every payment and pay check, leading to more financial clarity and peace of mind.

Setting Up Bill Reminders in Quicken

Staying on top of your bills is crucial for maintaining financial stability and avoiding late fees or penalties. Quicken makes it easy to manage your bill payments with its "Bill Reminder" feature. By setting up reminders, you ensure that you never miss a due date, giving you peace of mind and better control over your cash flow.

This step-by-step guide will walk you through the process of setting up bill reminders in Quicken, helping you automate and streamline your bill payments.

Why Set Up Bill Reminders?

Managing multiple bill payments manually can be time-consuming and risky, as missing a payment can lead to late fees, increased interest rates, or a hit to your credit score. Quicken's Bill Reminder feature allows you to:

- Stay on Track: Never miss a due date by receiving timely reminders for upcoming bills.
- Organize Your Payments: Track all of your bill payments in one place, whether they are utilities, rent, mortgage payments, credit card bills, or subscriptions.
- Manage Cash Flow: Plan ahead by knowing exactly when your bills are due and how much you need to pay, which helps you manage your cash flow more effectively.

Accessing the Bill Reminder Feature

To begin setting up bill reminders, you'll first need to navigate to the correct section of Quicken. Follow these steps to access the Bill Reminder feature:

Step 1:

Navigating to Bills & Income Tab

- Open Quicken: Launch the Quicken application on your computer.

- Go to Bills & Income Tab: From the main toolbar, click on the "Bills & Income" tab. This section houses all of the tools related to managing your bills and income.

Step 2:

Accessing the Manage Bill Reminders Section

- **Click on Manage Reminders:** In the Bills & Income tab, select "Manage Bill and Income Reminders". This will open a new window where you can view, add, edit, and manage all of your bill reminders.

Adding a New Bill Reminder

Now that you have accessed the Bill Reminder feature, you can begin adding your bills to the system. Here's how to add a new bill reminder:

Step 1:

Selecting Add Reminder

- Click Add Reminder: In the Manage Bill and Income Reminders window, click on the "Add Reminder button to start the process of setting up a new bill.
- Choose Bill Reminder: Quicken will prompt you to choose between setting up a "Bill Reminder" (for expenses) or an "Income Reminder". Select "Bill Reminder" to set up a reminder for upcoming payments.

Step 2:

Entering Bill Details

You will now need to input the details of the bill to ensure it's properly tracked.

- **Payee:** Enter the name of the payee, such as "Electric Company," "Water Utility," or "Credit Card."

- **Amount:** Enter the amount of the bill. If the amount is fixed (like rent or a loan payment), enter the exact figure. If the bill amount fluctuates (like utilities or credit card bills), you can estimate the amount or leave it blank and manually adjust it later.

- **Due Date:** Specify the next due date for the bill. Quicken will use this to schedule reminders.

- **Frequency:** Choose how often this bill recurs—monthly, quarterly, annually, or another custom frequency. For example, rent payments are typically monthly, while insurance premiums might be paid quarterly.

Step 3:

Setting a Reminder Date

To ensure that you receive timely notifications, set up the reminder date for the bill:

- Choose Reminder Lead Time: Select how far in advance you want to be reminded of the bill. For example, you might choose to be reminded 5 days before the bill is due, giving you enough time to make the payment.

- Save the Reminder: Once all the details are entered, click "OK" or "Save" to set up the bill reminder. The reminder will now appear in the Bills & Income section and will notify you at the specified time.

Managing and Editing Bill Reminders

Over time, you may need to update or modify your bill reminders as due dates or payment amounts change. Quicken makes it easy to edit or delete reminders as needed.

Step 1:

Viewing Bill Reminders

- Go to Bills & Income Tab: Navigate back to the "Bills & Income" tab to view your list of reminders.
- Check Due Dates and Status: In this section, you can see all upcoming bills, their due dates, and the status of each bill (whether it's been paid, is upcoming, or overdue).

Step 2:

Editing a Bill Reminder

- Select the Bill to Edit: To change the details of an existing reminder, click on the bill in the "Bills & Income" tab.
- Edit Details: Once selected, you can edit the payee name, amount, due date, or frequency of the bill.
- Save Changes: After making the necessary adjustments, click "Save" to update the bill reminder.

Step 3:

Deleting a Bill Reminder

- Select the Bill to Delete: If you no longer need a bill reminder (for example, if you've paid off a loan or cancelled a subscription), click on the bill in the Bills & Income tab.
- Delete the Reminder: Click on the "Delete" option to remove the bill reminder from Quicken. This will stop any future reminders for that particular bill.

Automating Bill Payments

For users who prefer to automate their bill payments, Quicken also offers an option to integrate your bill reminders with your bank's online bill pay system. This allows you to not only receive reminders but also automatically schedule payments, ensuring that your bills are paid on time.

Step 1:

Linking to Online Bill Pay

- Go to Bill Reminder: Open the bill reminder you've already set up.
- Enable Auto-Pay: If your bank supports online bill pay, you can set up auto-pay directly from the reminder. Quicken will then automatically initiate the payment based on the due date and the amount you've entered.
- Confirm Auto-Pay Setup: Confirm that the auto-pay feature is activated and that the bill will be paid without needing further manual intervention.

Step 2:

Tracking Auto-Paid Bills

- Monitor Payment Status: Quicken will update the status of auto-paid bills in the "Bills & Income" tab, showing you when a payment has been processed.

- Receive Notifications: Even for bills that are paid automatically, Quicken will still send you notifications confirming that the payment has been made, allowing you to keep track of your finances.

Receiving Bill Reminders and Notifications

Once your bill reminders are set up, you will receive notifications based on the schedule you've specified. Quicken offers flexibility in how these reminders are delivered.

Step 1:

Setting Notification Preferences

- Access Alerts and Notifications Settings: Go to the "Alerts & Notifications" settings in Quicken to customize how you receive reminders.

- Select Notification Method: Choose whether you want to receive reminders via in-app notifications, email, or both. You can also customize when these reminders are sent days or weeks before the due date.

Step 2:

Staying Informed

- Monitor Your Dashboard: Quickens dashboard will show a summary of all upcoming bill payments, including reminders that are approaching or overdue.

- Receive Email Alerts: If you've opted for email notifications, you will receive reminders directly in your inbox, giving you additional assurance that you won't miss a payment.

Tracking Invoices and Income in Quicken

Tracking invoices and income in Quicken is an essential aspect of managing your finances, particularly if you are self-employed, own a small business, or generate income through freelance work. By properly tracking your income and managing invoices, you can get a clear picture of your cash flow, stay on top of unpaid invoices, and simplify tax preparation. This step-by-step guide will walk you through how to track invoices and income in Quicken, ensuring that you stay organized and on top of your finances.

Understanding Income and Invoices in Quicken

Before diving into the specifics of tracking invoices and income, it's important to understand how Quicken handles these aspects:

- Invoices: Invoices in Quicken are used to track bills sent to clients or customers for products or services rendered. Proper tracking of invoices helps ensure that you get paid on time and can follow up on unpaid accounts.
- Income Tracking: Income tracking helps you record and categorize the money you receive from different sources. Whether it's salary, freelance payments, or business sales, accurately tracking income gives you a clearer picture of your financial health.

Creating and Sending Invoices in Quicken

Quicken makes it easy to create and send professional invoices to clients. This feature is particularly useful if you are a freelancer or small business owner looking to streamline your invoicing process.

Step 1:

Navigating to the Invoices Section

- Go to the Business Tab: If you are using Quicken Home & Business, you will have access to the "Business" tab at the top of the screen.
- Click on Invoices: In the Business tab, click on "Invoices" to open the invoicing section. Here, you can create, view, and manage invoices.

Step 2:

Creating an Invoice

- Click on Create Invoice: In the invoice management window, click on "Create Invoice" to start the process.
- Enter Client Information: Fill in the client's name, address, and any other necessary details. If you've previously worked with the client, you can select them from the list of existing contacts.
- Add Line Items: Add the products or services you are billing for. Include a description, quantity, rate, and total amount for each line item. Quicken will automatically calculate the subtotal and total based on the items listed.
- Add Invoice Date and Due Date: Specify the date of the invoice and the due date. Setting due dates is important for tracking payments and sending reminders if invoices go unpaid.

Step 3:

Customizing the Invoice

- Invoice Number: Quicken automatically assigns an invoice number, but you can edit this if needed. It's important to have a unique invoice number for each invoice for tracking purposes.

- Terms and Conditions: Add any relevant terms and conditions, such as payment terms or late fees, in the designated section.

- Save and Send: Once you've completed the invoice, click Save. You can also send the invoice directly to the client via email from within Quicken.

Tracking Invoice Status

Tracking the status of invoices is critical for maintaining positive cash flow. Quicken allows you to monitor whether invoices have been paid, are overdue, or are still pending.

Step 1:

Viewing Outstanding Invoices

- Open the Invoices Section: In the Business tab, navigate to the "Invoices" section.

- View Invoice Status: Quicken categorizes invoices based on their status "Paid", "Unpaid", "Overdue" making it easy to see which invoices require follow-up.

- Filter Invoices: Use the filter options to view invoices by date, client, or status, allowing you to get a quick overview of your outstanding invoices.

Step 2:

Sending Reminders for Overdue Invoices

If an invoice becomes overdue, it's important to follow up to ensure prompt payment.

- Select the Overdue Invoice: Click on any overdue invoice in the list to view the details.
- Send a Reminder: From the invoice detail page, click "Send Reminder". This option will send an automated email reminder to your client, including details of the overdue payment.

Step 3:

Marking Invoices as Paid

- Enter Payment Information: When a client pays an invoice, go to the invoice in the Invoices section and click "Mark as Paid".
- Record Payment Details: Enter the amount paid, the payment date, and the payment method (e.g., bank transfer, check, credit card). Quicken will automatically update your income records and mark the invoice as "Paid".

Tracking Income in Quicken

Accurately tracking income in Quicken helps you keep a clear picture of the money flowing into your accounts. It's essential for budgeting, planning, and tax preparation.

Step 1:

Recording Income from Invoices

When you mark an invoice as paid, Quicken will automatically record the income in the appropriate category. This makes it easy to keep track of your business earnings without manually entering the information twice.

Step 2:

Manually Adding Income

For income that doesn't originate from an invoice such as salary, freelance income, or other business revenue you can add the transaction manually.

- Go to the Account Register: Navigate to the account where you want to add the income. This could be your checking account or a business account.
- Click Add Transaction: Click "Add Transaction" to manually enter income.
- Enter the Income Details: Fill in the details, such as the date, payee (source of income), category (e.g., "Salary", "Freelance", "Rental Income"), and amount.
- Save the Transaction: Click "Save" to add the income to your account. This income will now be included in your overall financial overview and reports.

Step 3:

Categorizing and Tagging Income

- Categorize Income: Ensure each income transaction is assigned to the correct category. This makes it easy to see how much income is coming from different sources, such as "Freelance Projects", "Product Sales", or "Rental Income".
- Use Tags: You can also use tags to further organize income transactions. For example, if you have multiple freelance clients, use tags to indicate which client the income came from. This allows you to track income by client in your reports.

Generating Income Reports

Generating reports on your income is an important part of managing your finances, especially for small businesses and freelancers. Quicken provides tools to create income-specific reports that help you understand your financial position better.

Step 1:

Accessing Income Reports

- Go to the Reports Tab: Navigate to the "Reports" tab from the main toolbar.
- Select Income & Expense Reports: Click on "Income & Expense Reports" and select "Income by Category" or "Income Summary" to generate a report detailing your earnings.

Step 2:

Customizing Reports

- Filter by Date or Category: Use the filter options to narrow the report to a specific date range, client, or income category.
- Review Income Trends: Reviewing these reports regularly will help you identify trends in your earnings, track which clients or projects are most profitable, and make informed decisions about your finances.

CHAPTER SEVEN: INVESTING WITH QUICKEN

Investing can be one of the most powerful ways to build wealth, but it requires planning, tracking, and regular adjustments to achieve the best results. With Quicken, managing investments becomes more accessible and less time-consuming, allowing you to keep all your financial information in one place. Quickens investment features provide you with an organized, real-time view of your portfolio, so you can track performance, analyse trends, and make informed decisions.

Whether you're new to investing or an experienced trader, Quicken equips you with tools to monitor stocks, bonds, mutual funds, and other assets. Its easy-to-read charts, performance tracking, and automatic updates ensure you're always aware of where your investments stand. By combining these features with your overall financial data, Quicken helps you see the bigger picture, making it easier to align your investments with your personal goals. In this chapter, we'll guide you through the essentials of using Quicken for investment management, from tracking your first assets to gaining insights that help you maximize your returns. Let's explore how Quicken can empower you to invest smarter, grow your wealth, and achieve financial freedom.

Linking Your Investment Accounts in Quicken

Linking your investment accounts to Quicken is a crucial step in managing your portfolio effectively and understanding your overall financial health. By connecting your brokerage accounts, retirement accounts, and other investment holdings, you can track your investment performance, monitor gains or losses, and plan for future financial goals. Quicken makes it easy to link various types of investment accounts, allowing you to keep all of your financial data in one centralized platform. To get a full picture of your portfolio, linking your investment accounts in Quicken is a quick and essential first step. By connecting accounts like brokerage, retirement, and mutual funds, you can automatically import real-time data, eliminating the need for manual entries. Simply navigate to the "Add Account" feature, select the type of investment account, and enter your login credentials for secure access. Quicken will sync your holdings, transactions, and market values, providing a clear, updated view of your investments. With linked accounts, tracking your portfolio's performance becomes seamless, helping you stay informed and make data-driven decisions. Below is a step-by-step guide on how to link your investment accounts in Quicken. Here's a brief section on linking your investment accounts in Quicken:

Understanding the Benefits of Linking Investment Accounts

Linking your investment accounts in Quicken offers several key benefits:

I. **Real-Time Portfolio Tracking:** By connecting your investment accounts, you can track the value of your assets in real-time. Quicken automatically updates the current value of your investments, so you always have an up-to-date view of your portfolio.

II. **Investment Performance Analysis:** Quicken provides insights into the performance of your investments, including gains, losses, and rates of return. This helps you understand whether your investments are meeting your financial goals.

III. **Consolidated Financial Overview:** Linking your investment accounts allows you to view your entire financial picture in one place, including bank accounts, credit cards, and investments. This makes it easier to understand your net worth and plan for the future.

Preparing to Link Investment Accounts

Before linking your investment accounts to Quicken, ensure you have the following information ready:

I. Brokerage Account Credentials: You'll need your login information for each brokerage or investment account you want to link. This usually includes your username and password.

II. Account Type: Determine which types of accounts you are linking (e.g., retirement accounts like IRAs or 401(k)s, brokerage accounts, or mutual funds).

III. Investment Documents: Have your most recent account statements available to verify balances and account details if needed.

Linking an Investment Account to Quicken

Follow these steps to link your investment accounts to Quicken:

Step 1:

Navigate to the Add Account Section

- Go to the Account List: Open Quicken and navigate to the left-hand panel where your accounts are listed.

- Click on Add Account: At the top of the left panel, click "Add Account". This will open a new window where you can choose the type of account to link.

Step 2:

Select the Investment Account Type

- Choose Investment: In the Add Account window, you'll see different options for account types. Select "Investing & Retirement" to begin linking your brokerage or retirement accounts.

- Select Your Brokerage Firm: A list of popular brokerage firms will appear. You can either select your brokerage from the list or use the search bar to find it. For example, you might choose "Fidelity", "Vanguard", or "Charles Schwab".

Step 3:

Enter Account Credentials

- Enter Login Information: You will be prompted to enter the login credentials for your brokerage account. This information is required for Quicken to connect to your brokerage and download your investment data securely.

- Verify Your Identity: Depending on your brokerage's security settings, you may need to verify your identity. This could involve receiving a code via text, email, or through an authenticator app. Enter the verification code when prompted.

Importing Investment Data

Once your brokerage account credentials have been verified, Quicken will begin importing your investment data.

Step 1:

Select Accounts to Link

- View Available Accounts: After logging in, Quicken will display a list of available accounts associated with your brokerage firm. This could include brokerage accounts, IRAs, 401(k)s, or any other investment accounts held at that institution.
- Choose Accounts to Link: Select the accounts you want to link to Quicken. You can choose one or multiple accounts depending on what you need to track.
- Click Next: After selecting your accounts, click "Next" to begin importing the data.

Step 2:

Import Transactions and Holdings

- Import Investment Holdings: Quicken will import information about your current investment holdings, including the number of shares, market value, purchase prices, and any dividends received.
- Download Recent Transactions: In addition to importing your holdings, Quicken will also download recent transactions, such as buy/sell orders, dividend payments, and capital gains distributions.

Step 3:

Review and Confirm Account Setup

- Review Investment Data: After importing the data, Quicken will display a summary of your accounts, including current holdings and balances. Review this information to ensure everything matches your brokerage statements.

- Assign Categories (Optional): For certain transactions, you may want to assign specific categories (e.g., "Capital Gains," "Dividends"). This helps Quicken provide more detailed reports on your investment performance.

Viewing Linked Investment Accounts in Quicken

Once your investment accounts are linked, you can easily view and track your investment performance within Quicken.

Step 1:

Go to the Investing Tab

- Navigate to the Investing Tab: Click on the "Investing" tab from the main dashboard. This section provides an overview of all your linked investment accounts.

- View Portfolio Summary: In the Investing tab, you'll see a summary of your portfolio, including the total value, gains/losses, and individual holdings.

Step 2:

Review Individual Accounts

- Select Specific Accounts: From the left-hand panel, click on the name of any specific investment account to view more detailed information, such as individual transactions, performance metrics, and account balances.

- Check Performance Metrics: Quicken will provide performance metrics like daily changes, rate of return, and overall portfolio growth. This data helps you assess how well your investments are performing over time.

Maintaining and Updating Linked Investment Accounts

Your investment accounts will be updated automatically in Quicken whenever there is new activity or price changes. However, there are a few actions you can take to ensure your investment data stays accurate:

Step 1:

Update Your Accounts Regularly

- Use the Update Button: Quicken automatically updates your accounts daily, but you can manually update them by clicking the "Update" button at the top of the screen. This is particularly useful if you want to see the most recent price changes or transactions.
- Check for Sync Errors: If an account fails to update, check for sync errors. You may need to re-enter your credentials or verify your identity again, especially if your brokerage's security settings have changed.

Step 2:

Reconciling Investment Accounts

- Compare with Brokerage Statements: Periodically, it's a good idea to reconcile your investment accounts with your brokerage statements. This helps ensure the accuracy of your data, especially when there are complex transactions like dividend reinvestments or corporate actions (e.g., splits or mergers).

- Adjust as Necessary: If there are discrepancies between your Quicken records and your brokerage statements, adjust the balances or update the information to reflect the correct values.

Monitoring Your Net Worth in Quicken

Monitoring your net worth is one of the most effective ways to track your financial progress and gain a better understanding of your overall financial health. Net worth is the difference between your assets (what you own) and your liabilities (what you owe). By regularly monitoring your net worth in Quicken, you can see whether your financial decisions are helping you grow wealth or if adjustments are needed to improve your financial standing. This step-by-step guide will help you monitor your net worth using Quicken, leveraging the platform's tools to track, analyse, and improve your financial situation.

Understanding Net Worth

Net worth is a key financial metric that provides an overall picture of your wealth:

- **Assets:** Include everything you own, such as cash, real estate, investments, vehicles, and other valuable possessions. These are linked through Quicken accounts, such as checking savings, brokerage, or retirement accounts.
- **Liabilities:** Include everything you owe, such as mortgages, loans, credit card balances, and other debts. Quicken keeps track of these through linked accounts for credit cards, loans, and other liabilities.

By subtracting your liabilities from your assets, Quicken calculates your net worth, giving you a snapshot of your financial status.

Setting Up Accounts for Net Worth Tracking

To effectively monitor your net worth, it is important to link all of your financial accounts to Quicken. These accounts should include bank accounts, credit cards, loans, investment accounts, and any other assets or liabilities.

Step 1:

Link Your Accounts

- Go to the Add Account Section: Open Quicken and navigate to the left-hand panel. Click "Add Account" to link new financial accounts to Quicken.
- Add All Asset Accounts: Link all accounts that represent assets, such as checking, savings, and brokerage accounts, as well as the value of any real estate or vehicles you own.
- Add Liability Accounts: Link liability accounts, including credit cards, mortgages, auto loans, and any other debts you may have. This helps Quicken calculate your total liabilities accurately.

Step 2:

Manually Entering Assets and Liabilities

For assets that cannot be linked directly to a financial institution such as real estate or personal property you can manually enter these details:

- Add Manual Accounts: In the "Add Account" section, select "Manual Account" to add assets like real estate, jewellery, or vehicles.
- Enter Current Value: Provide an estimated value for each asset. You can update these values periodically as they change.

Viewing Your Net Worth in Quicken

Quicken offers a dedicated net worth tracking feature that makes it easy to see how your assets and liabilities balance out.

Step 1:

Navigate to the Net Worth Overview

- Open the Planning Tab: In the main menu, click on the "Planning" tab. This tab is where you can access budgeting tools, goals, and net worth information.
- Select Net Worth: Under the Planning tab, select "Net Worth" to view your financial summary. This section displays an overview of your total assets, liabilities, and net worth.

Step 2:

Viewing Net Worth Over Time

Quicken provides detailed charts and graphs that allow you to track how your net worth changes over time:

- Net Worth Chart: The "Net Worth Chart" shows a visual representation of your net worth growth or decline over a specified period. This helps you identify trends, such as steady growth or sudden drops, which may require further investigation.

- Custom Date Range: Use the date filter to select a specific time frame. For example, you can view changes in net worth over the past month, year, or several years. This flexibility helps you understand long-term trends in your financial health.

Analysing Your Net Worth

Monitoring your net worth is more meaningful when you take the time to analyse the contributing factors behind the changes. Quicken provides tools to help you drill down into the details.

Step 1:

Identifying Key Contributors

- View Account Balances: In the Net Worth section, Quicken breaks down your assets and liabilities by account. This makes it easy to see which accounts have contributed the most to changes in your net worth.
- Asset and Liability Analysis: Compare changes in asset values and liability balances. For example, an increase in net worth could be due to a rise in investment value or the reduction of debt.

Step 2:

Analyzing Cash Flow Impact

- Review Cash Flow Reports: Quicken provides cash flow reports that detail your income and expenses. Understanding how your cash flow affects your net worth helps you identify areas where you may need to adjust your spending or saving habits.

- Look for Patterns: Identify spending patterns or major expenses that may be holding back your net worth growth. This analysis can help you make better decisions to enhance your financial position.

Updating Asset Values

For a true reflection of your net worth, it's important to keep your asset values up-to-date, especially for assets that do not automatically update, like real estate or vehicles.

Step 1:

Manually Update Asset Values

- Go to the Account List: In the left-hand panel, select the asset account that needs updating, such as a real estate property or a vehicle.
- Edit the Value: Click on "Edit" or "Update Value" and enter the current value. For real estate, you can use an estimated market value based on recent sales in your area.

Step 2:

Setting Regular Reminders

To ensure that your net worth remains accurate, set reminders to update your asset values regularly:

- Use Quicken's Reminder Tool: Go to "Tools > Reminders" and set up a reminder to review and update asset values quarterly or annually.
- Link with Market Changes: For investment accounts, Quicken will automatically update values based on market changes. However, for manually

entered assets, it's important to update their values periodically based on external factors, like appraisals or market data.

Using Net Worth Data to Set Financial Goals

Understanding your net worth—essentially the total of what you own minus what you owe—is one of the most powerful insights you can gain in financial planning. This snapshot of your current financial position serves as a foundation for setting achievable goals, whether it's paying off debt, saving for a down payment, or planning for retirement. With Quicken, tracking your net worth over time becomes simple and visual, allowing you to see your progress and adjust your strategies. By regularly reviewing your net worth data, you can make informed decisions that align with both your short-term needs and long-term aspirations. In this section, we'll explore how to use Quickens net worth tracking to set meaningful, realistic. Tracking your net worth is not just about seeing where you stand—it's also about setting and achieving financial goals. By monitoring your net worth, you can plan how to improve your financial health over time.

Step 1:

Set Specific Goals

I.   Create Financial Goals in Quicken: Under the "Planning" tab, you can create financial goals such as "Saving for a Down Payment" or "Paying Off Debt".

II.   Align Goals with Net Worth Tracking: Ensure that your goals are contributing to net worth growth. For example, paying off debt directly improves your net worth by reducing liabilities.

Step 2:

Monitor Progress Toward Goals

- Track Goal Progress: Quicken will show your progress toward each financial goal, helping you stay motivated. This progress is also reflected in your net worth as your assets grow or liabilities decrease.

- Adjust as Needed: If you're not on track to meet a goal, review your budget or cash flow reports to identify areas where you can make adjustments, such as cutting expenses or allocating more money to savings.

Understanding Investment Reports

Investment reports are designed to provide a comprehensive overview of the status and performance of your investment portfolio. Quicken offers several types of investment reports that can help you answer questions such as:

- How are my investments performing over a specific period?
- What are my realized and unrealized gains or losses?
- How is my portfolio allocated across different asset classes?
- What dividends or interest income have I earned?

Using these reports, you can evaluate whether your investment strategy is effective and make adjustments as needed to align with your financial goals.

Accessing Investment Reports in Quicken

To create an investment report in Quicken, you need to navigate to the Reports section. Follow these steps to access investment reports:

Step 1:

Go to the Reports Menu

- **Navigate to the Reports Tab:** From the main dashboard, click on the "Reports" tab in the top toolbar. This will open the Reports menu, where you can access different types of financial reports.
- **Select Investing Reports:** Under the Reports menu, you will see a variety of report categories. Select "Investing" to see the different types of investment reports available.

Step 2:

Choose the Type of Investment Report

Quicken offers several types of investment reports that can help you analyze various aspects of your portfolio:

- **Portfolio Value Report:** Displays the value of your investments over a specific time frame, helping you track growth or decline in your portfolio.
- **Performance Report:** Shows the performance of individual investments, including gains, losses, and rate of return.
- **Income and Expense Report:** Summarizes income earned from investments, such as dividends and interest, as well as any related expenses.

- **Capital Gains Report:** Details realized and unrealized gains and losses, helping you understand the tax implications of your investments.
- **Asset Allocation Report:** Displays how your portfolio is allocated across different asset classes, such as stocks, bonds, and cash.

Choose the report that best suits your needs based on the information you want to analyse.

Customizing Investment Reports

Once you've selected the type of investment report you want to create, Quicken allows you to customize it to get the most relevant information for your situation. Customizing a report can help you focus on specific accounts, time periods, or types of investments.

Step 1:

Set the Date Range

- **Select the Date Range:** At the top of the report window, you will see options to adjust the date range. Choose a time frame that best suits your analysis— such as "Last Month", "Year to Date", or a "Custom Range".
- **Adjust for Historical Analysis:** To see how your investments have performed over a long period, select a multi-year date range. This helps you understand long-term trends in your portfolio performance.

Step 2:

Filter by Account or Security

- **Choose Accounts:** If you have multiple investment accounts, you can filter the report to include specific accounts. For example, you might want to create a report for just your retirement accounts (like an IRA or 401(k)) or for a taxable brokerage account.

- **Select Specific Securities:** You can also choose to include or exclude specific securities. For instance, you can create a report focusing only on stocks, bonds, or mutual funds to see how different types of investments are performing.

Step 3:

Adjust Report Categories

- **Include or Exclude Categories:** Depending on your goals, you may want to include specific categories of investments or expenses in the report. For example, if you're interested in understanding income from dividends, you can filter to focus on income categories only.

- **Group by Asset Class or Sector:** Some reports allow you to group data by asset class or investment sector, making it easier to see how your portfolio is diversified.

Interpreting Investment Reports

Once you've created an investment report, it's important to interpret the data effectively so you can make informed financial decisions. Here's how to interpret some of the key metrics found in investment reports:

Step 1:

Reviewing Portfolio Performance

- **Gains and Losses:** The "Performance Report" will show you realized and unrealized gains and losses for each investment. This helps you understand which investments have been successful and which may need re-evaluation.
- **Rate of Return:** The "Rate of Return" metric provides insight into the overall performance of your portfolio. Compare this rate against market benchmarks to assess whether your investments are meeting your expectations.

Step 2:

Analysing Income from Investments

- **Dividend and Interest Income:** The "Income and Expense Report" provides a summary of income generated from dividends, interest, and other sources. This is particularly useful for those who rely on investment income for cash flow.
- **Identify Consistent Income Sources:** Use this report to identify which investments provide consistent income and which are underperforming. This helps you make adjustments to maximize income potential.

Step 3:

Evaluating Asset Allocation

- **Review Asset Allocation Report:** The "Asset Allocation Report" shows the breakdown of your portfolio across different asset classes, such as stocks, bonds, and cash. Diversification is crucial for managing risk, and this report helps you determine if your portfolio is balanced appropriately for your risk tolerance.

- **Adjust Based on Risk:** If you notice that your portfolio is overly concentrated in a particular asset class, consider reallocating to achieve better diversification.

Step 4:

Planning for Taxes with Capital Gains Report

- **Capital Gains Report:** The "Capital Gains Report" helps you understand realized and unrealized gains and losses, which can impact your taxes. Reviewing this report before year-end can help you make tax-efficient decisions, such as selling underperforming investments to offset gains.

Saving and Exporting Investment Reports

After creating and customizing your investment report, Quicken allows you to save or export the report for future reference or for sharing with financial advisors.

Step 1:

Save the Report

- **Click Save:** At the top of the report window, click "Save" to store the customized report in Quicken. You can access saved reports at any time from the "Reports" menu.
- **Name Your Report:** Assign a unique name to the report so you can easily identify it later, such as "Year-to-Date Portfolio Performance" or "Monthly Dividend Income."

Step 2:

Export the Report

- **Export to PDF or Excel:** If you need to share the report or keep a copy for offline access, click "Export" to save the report as a PDF or Excel file. This feature is useful if you want to share the report with your financial advisor or keep a hard copy for your records.

- **Email the Report:** Quicken also provides the option to email the report directly if needed, making it easy to communicate with others about your investment performance.

CHAPTER EIGHT: GETTING READY FOR TAXES

Tax season can be stressful, but with Quicken, preparing for taxes becomes a much simpler and more organized process. Whether you're filing as an individual, self-employed, or managing investment income, Quicken helps you track and categorize all your financial data, so you can easily prepare for tax time without the last-minute rush.

1. Organizing Your Tax Documents

Quicken allows you to categorize all your expenses, income, and deductions throughout the year. By using categories like "Taxes," "Medical," and "Charitable Donations," you can quickly pull up relevant data when it's time to file your tax return. This means you won't have to sift through piles of receipts or documents at the last minute—you'll already have everything neatly organized and ready to go.

2. Tracking Tax-Deductible Expenses

Quickens built-in tax features make it easy to track tax-deductible expenses, such as business expenses, home office costs, and medical expenses. By entering these expenses throughout the year, you'll be able to accurately calculate deductions and reduce your taxable income when it's time to file. Quickens reports can help you identify which expenses are deductible and give you a clearer picture of your tax liability.

3. Preparing Investment Data for Tax Filing

If you have investments, Quicken makes it easy to generate reports on capital gains, dividends, and interest income. These reports can be directly imported into tax preparation software or shared with your accountant, saving you time and reducing the risk of errors. Quickens accurate tracking ensures that you don't miss any important income or deductions related to your investments.

4. Creating Tax Reports

Quickens tax-related reports are designed to simplify the tax preparation process. You can generate reports that summarize income, expenses, and deductions, giving you a comprehensive view of your finances. These reports can be used to assist in filling out your tax return or provide valuable information to your tax professional.

5. Connecting to TurboTax or Tax Software

For even more convenience, Quicken integrates seamlessly with TurboTax and other tax software. You can export your financial data directly from Quicken, reducing the need for manual data entry. This integration ensures that your tax filing is accurate and efficient, helping you avoid mistakes and potential audits.

By staying organized throughout the year with Quicken, you'll have everything you need at tax time, making the process less stressful and more manageable. Whether you're filing simple personal taxes or managing a complex investment portfolio, Quicken provides the tools to help you get ready for taxes with confidence.

Tracking Deductible Expense

Tracking deductible expenses is a crucial part of managing your finances, especially if you're self-employed, own a small business, or want to maximize your tax deductions. Quicken makes it easy to track expenses, categorize them appropriately, and generate reports that simplify tax preparation. By accurately tracking your deductible expenses, you can ensure you're taking full advantage of tax savings opportunities while also keeping organized records. This step-by-step guide will walk you through how to effectively track deductible expenses in Quicken.

Understanding Deductible Expenses

Deductible expenses are those that can be subtracted from your income before calculating taxes, reducing the total amount you owe. These expenses vary depending on your situation and may include:

- **Business Expenses:** Costs related to running a business, such as office supplies, travel, utilities, and advertising.
- **Medical Expenses:** Qualified medical expenses that exceed a certain percentage of your income.
- **Charitable Donations:** Contributions to qualifying non-profit organizations.
- **Home Office Expenses:** If you use a portion of your home for business purposes, you may be able to deduct related expenses.

- **Educational Expenses:** Qualified educational costs, such as tuition for career-related courses.

Quickens tools make it easy to keep track of these expenses, categorize them, and generate tax reports.

Setting Up Categories for Deductible Expenses

The first step in effectively tracking deductible expenses is to set up categories that align with your tax deductions. Quicken allows you to customize categories, which helps you accurately track and organize deductible expenses for tax reporting.

Step 1:

Access the Category List

- **Navigate to the Tools Menu:** Click on "Tools" in the top menu bar, then select "Category List". This will open a list of all categories that are currently in use in your Quicken file.
- **Review Existing Categories:** Quicken comes with a range of default categories, such as "Medical", "Charity", "Office Supplies", and "Utilities". Review these categories to see if they fit your needs.

Step 2:

Adding or Customizing Categories

- **Create a New Category:** If a category you need is not already available, click on "New Category". Enter a name that describes the deductible expense such as "Marketing Costs" or "Medical Deductions."

- **Assign to Tax-Deductible Group:** While creating the category, make sure to mark it as "Tax-Related" by checking the appropriate box. This ensures that the category will appear in Quickens tax reports, making tax preparation easier.

- **Add Subcategories:** To further organize your deductible expenses, you can add subcategories. For instance, under "Business Expenses," you could create subcategories like "Travel," "Supplies," and "Meals & Entertainment."

Tracking Deductible Expenses in the Account Register

After setting up your categories, the next step is to track deductible expenses by entering them into your account registers. Whether you are manually entering expenses or downloading them from linked accounts, it's important to assign each transaction to the correct category.

Step 1:

Entering Transactions Manually

- **Go to the Account Register:** Open the account register where the expense was incurred (e.g., checking account, credit card).

- **Add a New Transaction:** Click "Add Transaction" or "Enter Transaction" at the top of the register to add a new expense manually.

- **Fill in Transaction Details:** Enter the "Date", "Payee", "Amount", and most importantly assign the appropriate "Category". Choose a category that matches the deductible expense, such as "Medical Expenses" or "Office Supplies."

- **Add Notes or Tags:** To make the expense easier to identify later, add notes or tags. For example, if you're entering a charitable donation, you could add a note indicating the organization's name and the purpose of the donation.

Step 2:

Downloading Transactions from Linked Accounts

If your bank accounts or credit cards are linked to Quicken, transactions will be downloaded automatically. You can then categorize these transactions as deductible expenses:

- **Review Downloaded Transactions:** Go through your account register to review downloaded transactions. Quicken may automatically assign categories, but it's important to verify that they are correct.
- **Edit Categories:** Click on the category field for any transaction that is deductible and assign the appropriate tax-related category. If a business lunch is categorized as "Dining," change it to "Meals & Entertainment (Tax Deductible)."

Using Tags for Better Organization

Tags can add an additional layer of organization to your deductible expenses. Tags help you track specific projects, clients, or events that are linked to expenses across multiple categories.

Step 1:

Adding Tags to Transactions

- **Open the Transaction:** Click on the transaction in the account register to view its details.

- **Enter the Tag:** In the "Tags" field, enter a tag that identifies the expense. For instance, if you are tracking expenses related to a specific project or client, you could use a tag like "Project A" or "Client B."

- **Save the Transaction:** Once the tag has been added, save the transaction. You can use tags in your reports to filter and analyse expenses related to specific projects or events.

Step 2:

Managing Tags

- Open the Tag List: To manage tags, go to "Tools > Tag List". Here, you can create, edit, or delete tags as needed.

- Group Related Expenses: Tags make it easy to group related expenses for analysis. For example, if you tag all marketing-related expenses, you can quickly see how much you're spending on marketing in a given period.

Generating Reports for Tax Preparation

Quickens reporting feature makes it easy to generate a summary of deductible expenses, making tax preparation much simpler.

Step 1:

Create a Tax Report

- **Navigate to the Reports Tab:** From the main menu, click on the "Reports" tab.

- **Select Tax Reports:** Under the Reports menu, choose "Tax" to access tax-related reports. Select the "Schedule A (Itemized Deductions)" report or "Tax Summary Report" to see a breakdown of your deductible expenses.

Step 2:

Customize the Report

- **Filter by Date Range:** Set the date range for the report to cover the relevant tax year. This ensures you are only seeing expenses that apply to the current filing period.
- **Review the Report:** Quicken will generate a report showing all deductible expenses categorized by type. Review the report to ensure all transactions are correctly categorized, and no expenses are missing.

Step 3:

Export or Print the Report

- **Save for Tax Filing:** You can save the report as a PDF or export it to Excel to share with your accountant or keep for your records.
- **Print the Report:** If needed, print the report for reference during tax preparation. Having a printed copy makes it easier to discuss details with your tax advisor.

Setting Reminders for Recurring Deductible Expenses

To ensure you don't miss out on tracking regular deductible expenses, set up reminders in Quicken for recurring payments such as monthly charitable donations or quarterly tax payments.

Step 1:

Set Up a Reminder

- **Navigate to Bill and Income Reminders:** Go to "Tools > Manage Bill & Income Reminders".

- **Add a New Reminder:** Click on "Add Reminder" and fill in the details for the recurring deductible expense.

- **Assign a Category:** Assign the correct category to the expense, such as "Charity" or "Estimated Tax Payments," to ensure it's tracked as deductible.

Step 2:

Track and Confirm

- **Check the Reminder:** Each time a reminder comes up, verify that the payment is recorded in the correct category.

- **Confirm the Transaction:** Mark the reminder as paid in Quicken, ensuring it's reflected in your account register and included in your deductible expenses.

Tagging Tax-Deductible Expenses in Quicken

Tagging tax-deductible expenses in Quicken is an effective way to ensure your financial records are well-organized, allowing you to easily track and categorize deductible items such as charitable contributions, medical bills, mortgage interest, and more. By using tags, you create an additional layer of classification beyond standard categories, which is especially useful when preparing for taxes. This guide will show you how to tag tax-deductible expenses in Quicken, making it easier to generate accurate tax reports and maximize your deductions.

Understanding Tags in Quicken

Tags are labels you can assign to transactions to further categorize or group them, offering an extra layer of organization beyond the default categories. This feature is particularly helpful for:

- **Grouping Expenses:** You can group related tax-deductible expenses by tagging them with a specific label, such as "Charity" or "Medical."

- **Filtering Reports:** Tags make it easier to filter and analyse transactions, especially when running tax reports or reviewing expenses related to a specific project or purpose.

- **Better Record Keeping:** Tags allow for detailed tracking, ensuring no deductible expenses are missed during tax preparation.

Setting Up Tags for Tax-Deductible Expenses

Before you begin tagging transactions, it's important to set up relevant tags for all types of tax-deductible expenses. This helps you accurately track deductions like charitable donations, medical expenses, and mortgage interest.

Step 1:

Access the Tag List

- **Navigate to Tools > Tag List:** In Quicken, go to "Tools" and then "Tag List". This will open a window where you can manage all tags in your Quicken file.

- **Create New Tags:** To create a new tag, click "New Tag". You can add tags for each type of tax-deductible expense you want to track. Common tags include:

  - ➢ Charity: Use this tag for all charitable contributions, donations, or gifts that are eligible for deduction.
  - ➢ Medical Bills: Use this tag for medical and dental expenses that may be deductible if they exceed a certain threshold of your income.
  - ➢ Mortgage Interest: This tag is used to track mortgage interest payments, which are often tax-deductible.

Step 2:

Customize Tags for Specific Needs

- **Add Descriptions (Optional):** You can add a description to each tag to make it clear what it's used for. For example, you could add a note to the "Medical Bills" tag to remind you that only out-of-pocket expenses count toward the deduction.
- **Organize Tags:** Keep your tags organized by grouping related tags together. This makes it easier to select them when entering transactions.

Tagging Tax-Deductible Transactions

Once your tags are set up, you can begin tagging transactions that qualify as tax-deductible. This can be done either when manually entering transactions or reviewing downloaded transactions.

Step 1:

Entering a Tagged Transaction Manually

- **Navigate to the Account Register:** Open the account register where the expense occurred, such as your checking account or credit card.

- **Add a New Transaction:** Click "Add Transaction" to enter a new expense.

- **Assign a Category:** Choose the appropriate category for the expense, such as "Medical Expenses" or "Charity". This ensures the transaction is tracked as tax-deductible.

- **Add the Tag:** In the "Tags" field, enter the relevant tag. For example, if it's a charitable donation, type "Charity" to label the transaction as such.

- **Save the Transaction:** Once all the details are entered, click "Save" to store the transaction.

Step 2:

Tagging Downloaded Transactions

If your accounts are linked to Quicken, transactions will be automatically downloaded. It's important to review these transactions and apply the correct tags to any that qualify as tax-deductible.

- **Review Downloaded Transactions:** Open the account register and review all downloaded transactions.

- **Identify Tax-Deductible Expenses:** Look for any transactions that qualify for deductions, such as donations, medical payments, or mortgage interest.

- **Add Tags to Transactions:** Click on the transaction, and in the "Tags" field, enter the tag that matches the type of deduction, such as "Medical Bills" or "Mortgage Interest."

- **Save Changes:** Once the tag is added, save the transaction to ensure it is properly labelled.

Using Tags in Tax Reports

Tags make it easy to generate tax reports that include all of your deductible expenses. This can simplify tax preparation and ensure that no deduction is overlooked.

Step 1:

Generating a Tax Report

- **Navigate to the Reports Tab:** Click on the "Reports" tab from the main menu.

- **Select Tax Reports:** Under the "Tax" category, select Tax Summary Report or Schedule A: Itemized Deductions Report. These reports show all transactions categorized as tax-related.

Step 2:

Filtering by Tags

- **Customize the Report:** In the report settings, use the "Filter by Tags" option to include only specific tags in the report. For example, you can generate a report that shows only transactions tagged as "Charity" or "Medical Bills."

- **Review and Analyse:** Reviewing reports filtered by tags allows you to see the total amounts for each type of deduction, helping you ensure that all qualifying expenses are properly accounted for.

Step 3:

Export or Print the Report

- **Save or Export the Report:** Save the report as a PDF or export it to Excel for tax preparation. This is helpful for sharing with an accountant or keeping a record of all deductions.

- **Print the Report:** If you prefer, print a hard copy to have on hand during tax filing, making it easy to reference and verify the information.

Benefits of Using Tags for Tax-Deductible Items

Using tags in Quicken to label tax-deductible items offers several key advantages:

- **Improved Organization:** Tags make it easier to group and identify tax-deductible expenses across different categories. This can be especially helpful for expenses that span multiple types, such as business travel or medical expenses.

- **Efficient Tax Preparation:** By tagging all deductible transactions, you simplify tax preparation, reducing the time and effort required to find eligible deductions.

- **Better Insights:** Tags allow for more detailed analysis of your spending, helping you understand how much you're spending on different types of deductible expenses and allowing you to plan better for tax savings.

Exporting Tax Documents in Quicken

Exporting tax documents from Quicken is a crucial step in preparing your financial information for tax filing. By exporting the relevant data, you can easily share it with your tax preparer or import it into tax software, ensuring a smooth and accurate tax filing process. Quicken makes exporting tax-related reports simple, allowing you to compile and present all necessary information in formats that are easy to manage. This guide will walk you through how to export tax documents from Quicken step-by-step.

Understanding the Importance of Exporting Tax Documents

Exporting tax documents allows you to:

- **Provide Records to Accountants:** If you're working with an accountant or tax professional, exporting documents from Quicken allows you to share detailed financial information easily.
- **Prepare for Tax Filing:** Exported reports can be used to verify income, deductions, and other tax-related details when preparing your tax return.
- **Maintain Records:** Keeping exported copies of tax documents allows you to have backup records in case of audits or for future reference.

Generating Tax Reports for Export

Before exporting, you need to generate the specific tax-related reports you'll be exporting. Quicken provides a variety of tax reports that can include income, expenses, deductions, and other financial details.

Step 1:

Navigate to the Reports Section

- **Go to the Reports Tab:** From the main dashboard, click on the "Reports" tab at the top of the screen.

- **Select Tax Reports:** Under the "Tax" category, you will find several relevant tax-related reports, such as "Tax Summary", "Tax Schedule", or "Schedule A Itemized Deductions". Choose the report that includes the information you need to export.

Step 2:

Customize the Report

- **Set the Date Range:** Adjust the date range to cover the tax year for which you are filing, such as "Last Year" or "Custom Range."
- **Filter Categories:** Review and, if needed, filter out irrelevant categories or include only specific ones, such as those related to charitable donations or business expenses.
- **review the Report:** After making all necessary adjustments, preview the report to ensure it includes all required information.

Exporting Tax Documents in Quicken

Once the report is generated and customized, the next step is to export it. Quicken provides several formats for exporting, such as PDF or Excel, which makes it easy to share or save the information.

Step 1:

Select the Export Option

- **Click on Export:** In the top right corner of the report, click on the "Export" button. This will display a drop-down menu with different export options.
- **Choose the Format:** You can export your report in either "PDF" or "Excel" format:

- ➤ PDF: Best for sharing with an accountant or for storing in a format that cannot be easily modified.

- ➤ Excel: Ideal for editing, analysing, or importing into tax preparation software.

Step 2:

Save the Exported File

- **Choose a Location:** After selecting the format, you'll be prompted to choose where you want to save the exported file on your computer. It's best to save it in a location that is easy to remember and access, such as a dedicated tax folder.

- **Name the File:** Use a clear and descriptive file name, such as "Tax_Summary_2023" or "Schedule_A_2023," to easily identify the document.

- **Click Save:** After naming the file, click "Save" to complete the export process.

Reviewing and Organizing Exported Documents

After exporting the tax documents, it's important to review them for accuracy and keep them organized. This will make it easier when preparing your tax return or when sharing information with your accountant.

Step 1:

Review the Exported File

- **Open the File:** Locate the exported file on your computer and open it to verify that all the necessary data has been captured.

- **Check for Completeness:** Review the content to make sure all income, deductions, and expenses are accurately represented. This is crucial to ensure that your tax return is accurate.

Step 2:

Organize Exported Files

- **Create a Tax Folder:** Create a folder on your computer named "Tax Documents [Year]" and save all exported reports in this folder. This helps you maintain an organized record of all your tax-related information.
- **Backup the Folder:** Save a backup copy of the folder to an external drive or cloud storage. This ensures that you have a secure copy in case of computer failure or other issues.

Preparing Your Expense Report in Quicken

Before exporting your expense report to TurboTax, you need to ensure that your Quicken records are up-to-date and accurately categorized. Proper categorization is essential for TurboTax to correctly classify your expenses as tax deductions.

Step 1:

Update Your Accounts

- **Link and Update Accounts:** Make sure all your accounts are linked and up-to-date in Quicken. This includes bank accounts, credit cards, and any other accounts used for deductible expenses.

- **Review Transactions:** Review all transactions for the tax year to ensure they are categorized correctly, such as "Charity", "Medical Expenses", or "Business Supplies.

Step 2:

Generate the Expense Report

- **Navigate to Reports > Spending:** In Quicken, click on the "Reports" tab, then select "Spending".
- **Select the Date Range:** Choose the tax year for which you want to generate the expense report.
- Customize Categories: Ensure that all tax-deductible categories are included in the report. This may include medical expenses, charitable contributions, and home office expenses.

Exporting the Expense Report

Once you've generated and reviewed your expense report, the next step is to export it in a format that TurboTax can import.

Step 1:

Exporting the File

- **Select Export:** Click on the "Export" button in the top right corner of the report window.
- **Choose the Format:** Select "Tax Export (TXF)". This format is specifically used for importing financial data into tax software like TurboTax.
- Save the File: Choose a location on your computer to save the exported file. It's best to save it in a folder labelled "Tax Documents" for easy access later.

Step 2:

Verify the Exported File

- **Open the Exported File:** Open the exported TXF file to ensure that it contains all relevant expense data. This step ensures that nothing was missed during the export process.
- **Check for Completeness:** Verify that all expenses, including deductions, are listed correctly. This helps avoid any potential discrepancies when importing into TurboTax.

Importing the Expense Report into TurboTax

With your expense report exported from Quicken, the next step is to import it into TurboTax. TurboTax makes it easy to bring in data from Quicken, reducing the manual work involved in tax preparation.

Step 1:

Open TurboTax

- **Launch TurboTax:** Open TurboTax on your computer and begin or continue your tax return.
- **Select Import Options:** Navigate to the "Import" section of TurboTax. Typically, TurboTax will prompt you to import financial data when setting up your tax return.

Step 2:

Import the TXF File

- **Select Quicken Import:** In the import options, select "Quicken (TXF)" to start importing your data.

- **Locate the File:** Browse your computer to locate the TXF file you exported from Quicken. Select the file and click "Open" to start the import.

- **Follow the Prompts:** TurboTax will guide you through the process of importing your data. Confirm that the information being imported is correct and matches the expense report generated in Quicken.

Step 3:

Review Imported Data

- **Review the Imported Expenses:** Once the data is imported, review the expense categories in TurboTax to ensure everything has been accurately transferred. Look for any missing or incorrectly classified entries.

- **Make Adjustments if Needed:** If TurboTax identifies any discrepancies or suggests adjustments, make the necessary changes to ensure your tax return is accurate.

Finalizing Your Tax Return

After importing and reviewing the expense report, finalize your tax return in TurboTax by including any additional information that may be required.

Step 1:

Complete the Tax Return

- **Add Any Additional Deductions:** If there are deductions or expenses not captured in Quicken, manually enter them into TurboTax.

- **Verify All Information:** Double-check that all imported data aligns with your financial records for the tax year, ensuring that your expenses and deductions are accurate.

Step 2:

File Your Tax Return

- **Use TurboTax's Error Check:** Before filing, use TurboTax's built-in error check to identify any potential mistakes.
- **Submit Your Tax Return:** Once everything is verified, submit your tax return electronically via TurboTax.

Benefits of Exporting Expense Reports to TurboTax

Exporting your expense reports from Quicken to TurboTax offers several benefits:

- **Saves Time:** Automating the data transfer from Quicken to TurboTax saves significant time, eliminating the need for manual entry.
- **Reduces Errors:** Exporting data minimizes the chances of human error during data entry, ensuring greater accuracy in your tax return.
- Maximizes Deductions: By ensuring that all deductible expenses are properly imported and categorized, you can maximize the deductions available to you, potentially reducing your tax liability.

Year-End Tax Preparation Tips Using Quicken

Year-end tax preparation can be a daunting task but using Quicken can simplify the process and help you get organized before tax season. Quickens tools and features make it easier to track expenses, categorize deductions, and generate tax-related reports. To maximize your tax deductions and reduce your tax liability, it's important to use Quicken effectively as you close out the year. Below are some essential year-end tax preparation tips for using Quicken.

Review and Update Your Accounts

To ensure that your financial data is accurate for tax purposes, review all linked accounts in Quicken. It's important to make sure that your transactions are correctly categorized and up-to-date.

Step 1:

Reconcile Your Accounts

- **Reconcile Bank and Credit Card Accounts:** Make sure that your bank, credit card, and other financial accounts are fully reconciled with your most recent statements. This ensures that all transactions are accurately recorded.
- **Verify Account Balances:** Compare the balances in Quicken with the statements from your financial institutions to ensure they match. Discrepancies should be addressed immediately.

Step 2:

Update Missing Transactions

- **Enter Missing Transactions:** Check for any missing transactions, such as cash payments, business expenses, or charitable contributions, and add them to your account register.

- **Categorize All Transactions:** Ensure that all transactions are correctly categorized, especially those that are tax-deductible, such as "Medical Expenses", "Charitable Donations", and "Home Office Expenses".

Organize and Categorize Tax-Deductible Expenses

Proper categorization of expenses is crucial for identifying eligible tax deductions. Quicken allows you to categorize expenses to streamline the process.

Step 1:

Create Custom Categories for Deductions

- **Customize Categories:** In Quicken, create custom categories for any unique tax-deductible expenses that may not be covered by default categories. This ensures accurate tracking for deductions like "Continuing Education Costs" or "Business Supplies".

- **Mark Categories as Tax-Related:** When setting up a category, mark it as "Tax-Related" by checking the appropriate box. Assigning tax line items to each category helps generate accurate tax reports.

Step 2:

Review and Update Categories

- **Review Categorized Transactions:** Go through all transactions to ensure they have been assigned the correct categories. For example, make sure all charitable contributions are under the "Charity" category.

- **Correct Mistakes:** If any transactions are miscategorized, correct them. Misclassified expenses can lead to inaccurate tax reports and missed deductions.

Track and Label Tax-Deductible Items with Tags

Tags in Quicken provide an additional layer of organization for your tax-deductible expenses, making it easier to find specific deductions.

Step 1:

Use Tags to Label Tax-Deductible Expenses

- **Add Tags to Transactions:** Tags can be used to label specific tax-deductible items, such as "Medical Bills" or "Business Travel". This makes it easy to group and review expenses related to certain deductions.

- **Create Consistent Tags:** Maintain consistent tag names for easier reference. For example, use "Medical" for all medical-related expenses and "Charity" for charitable donations.

Step 2:

Use Tags to Filter Reports

- **Generate Tax Reports by Tags:** Use tags to filter and generate reports of specific deductible expenses. This can be helpful for identifying areas that require further review or documentation.

- **Review Tagged Items for Accuracy:** Ensure that all tagged items are labelled correctly and qualify for deductions. This helps reduce confusion during tax preparation.

Generate Tax Reports for Review

Generating tax reports is an essential step in year-end tax preparation. Quicken provides several useful tax-related reports that can help you organize your data.

Step 1:

Create a Tax Summary Report

- **Go to Reports > Tax:** Click on the "Reports" tab and select "Tax" from the available report options.
- **Generate a Tax Summary Report:** Select the "Tax Summary Report" to see a summary of all tax-related transactions categorized by type, such as "Income", "Deductions", and "Credits".
- **Set the Date Range:** Adjust the date range to cover the entire tax year, such as January 1 to December 31.

Step 2:

Review the Report for Completeness

- **Check Deductions and Credits:** Review all deductions and credits listed in the report. Ensure that no deductible expenses have been missed, such as charitable contributions or medical expenses.
- **Compare to Bank Statements:** Cross-reference the information in the tax report with your bank and credit card statements to ensure that all transactions are recorded.

Export Tax Reports to Tax Software

Exporting your tax reports to tax software, such as TurboTax, can save time and reduce errors when preparing your tax return.

Step 1:

Export Reports in Tax Format

- **Export Tax Reports as TXF:** Click "Export" in the top right corner of the report window and choose "Tax Export (TXF)". This format is compatible with tax preparation software like TurboTax.
- **Save the File:** Save the exported file in a designated folder for tax documents to ensure easy access when preparing your taxes.

Step 2:

Import Data into TurboTax

- **Open TurboTax:** Launch TurboTax on your computer and navigate to the "Import" section.
- **Import Quicken Data:** Select "Import from Quicken" and locate the TXF file. Follow the prompts to complete the import and verify the data.

Ensure All Documentation Is Complete

Year-end tax preparation requires detailed documentation, especially for deductions that require proof, such as charitable donations or business expenses.

Step 1:

Attach Receipts and Statements

- **Attach Digital Receipts in Quicken:** Quicken allows you to attach digital copies of receipts to transactions. Attach receipts for all tax-deductible items, such as charitable contributions and medical bills.

- **Organize Receipts in a Folder:** Keep physical or digital copies of all receipts organized in a dedicated folder labelled "Tax Year [Year] for easy access.

Step 2:

Maintain Supporting Documents

- **Charitable Donation Receipts:** Ensure you have receipts or confirmation letters for all charitable donations. These are required to support deductions.

- **Business Expense Logs:** If you are self-employed, maintain detailed logs of business expenses, including travel, meals, and supplies. Quicken can help organize these logs for easy reference.

Plan for the Next Year

Taking steps to prepare for the upcoming year can make next year's tax preparation even smoother.

Step 1:

Review Spending Patterns

- **Analyse Tax Reports:** Review your tax reports to identify trends and spending patterns. This can help you adjust your financial strategy for the upcoming year.

- **Set Tax-Related Goals:** Based on your review, set goals for the upcoming year, such as increasing charitable donations or maximizing retirement contributions.

Step 2:

Set Up Recurring Reminders

- **Use Bill and Income Reminders:** Set up reminders in Quicken for recurring tax-related payments, such as estimated tax payments or charitable contributions.
- **Automate Expense Tracking:** Automate tracking for regular expenses to ensure they are accurately categorized and tagged throughout the year, reducing the year-end workload.

CHAPTER NINE: QUICKEN FOR SMALL BUISNESS OWNERS

As a small business owner, managing finances can be overwhelming. From tracking expenses and paying bills to handling payroll and filing taxes, the financial responsibilities are endless. This is where Quicken comes in. With its robust set of tools designed specifically for small business owners, Quicken simplifies the complexity of managing your business's finances, so you can focus on what you do best—growing your business. Quicken offers an all-in-one solution to help you track income and expenses, manage invoices, and even generate profit-and-loss reports. Whether you're just starting out or looking to streamline your financial processes, Quicken provides the tools to keep your business on track, compliant, and profitable. In this section, we'll explore how Quickens features can help you stay on top of your small business's financial needs, improve cash flow, and ensure that you're making the most of every dollar. From managing business expenses to preparing for tax season, Quicken helps you keep your financials in order with ease and confidence.

Setting Up Business Accounts

Setting up business accounts in Quicken is the foundational step for effectively managing your business finances. Whether you're running a small business or working as a freelancer, Quicken allows you to create separate accounts for tracking income, expenses, and other financial activities specific to your business. This separation helps streamline financial management, provides clear insights into your business performance, and ensures that your records are organized for tax purposes. Here's a detailed guide on how to set up business accounts in Quicken.

Setting Up a New Business Account in Quicken

To begin setting up your business accounts in Quicken, you'll need to add a new account specifically for business purposes. This account can be for tracking income, expenses, loans, or other financial activities related to your business.

Step 1:

Open the Add Account Wizard

- **Navigate to the Accounts Section:** In Quicken, click on the "Tools" menu and select "Add Account". This will open the Add Account Wizard.
- **Select Account Type:** You'll be prompted to select the type of account you want to create. Choose Business from the list of available options.

Step 2:

Choose the Type of Business Account

- **Select the Specific Account Type:** Quicken provides various types of accounts to suit your business needs. Select the type of business account you need, such as:
  - ➢ Checking or Savings: For tracking business-related bank transactions.
  - ➢ Credit Card: For recording business expenses paid by credit card.
  - ➢ Accounts Receivable: For tracking income that customers owe to your business.

> ➢ Loan or Liability Account: To keep track of business loans and their repayments.

- Link or Set Up Manually: You can either link the account to your bank for automatic transaction downloads or create a manual account for business transactions you enter yourself.

Configuring Business Account Settings

After adding the business account, it's important to configure it properly to ensure accurate tracking of your business finances.

Step 1:

Enter Account Details

- **Account Name:** Provide a name for your business account that will help you identify it easily, such as "Business Checking" or "Client Payments." Clear and descriptive names are key to staying organized.

- **Enter Account Information:** If you're linking the account to your bank, enter your bank login credentials to sync it with Quicken. For manual accounts, input the current balance and account details as of the date you're setting it up.

Step 2:

Set Up Categories for Business Transactions

- **Create Business Categories:** To track different types of business expenses and income effectively, Quicken allows you to create custom categories. For example, you can set up categories for "Office Supplies", "Client Payments", "Marketing Expenses", and "Travel".

- **Mark Categories as Business-Related:** Make sure that all categories you create for this account are marked as "Business" so they can be easily included in your financial reports.

Adding and Categorizing Business Transactions

Once your business accounts are set up, you can start adding and categorizing transactions to effectively track your business income and expenses.

Step 1:

Add Transactions Manually or Download Automatically

- **Download Transactions from Linked Accounts:** If you linked your business account to a bank, Quicken will automatically download recent transactions. Review these transactions to ensure they're categorized properly.
- **Enter Transactions Manually:** For cash payments or accounts that aren't linked, you'll need to enter transactions manually. Go to the "Account Register", click "Add Transaction", and input the date, payee, amount, and category.

Step 2:

Categorize Business Expenses

- **Assign Categories:** Assign each expense to a relevant category, such as "Advertising", "Rent", or "Travel Expenses". Proper categorization ensures that you can track where your money is going and identify areas for cost control.

- **Use Tags for Additional Detail:** You can also add tags to categorize transactions related to specific projects or clients, which allows you to generate reports based on tags to see how much you're spending or earning on a particular project.

Maintaining Your Business Accounts in Quicken

Setting up your business accounts is only the first step; consistent maintenance is key to keeping your business finances in order.

Step 1:

Update Regularly

- **Review Transactions Weekly:** Make it a habit to review and categorize transactions weekly. This practice keeps your records up-to-date and ensures you always have a clear view of your finances.
- **Reconcile Accounts Monthly:** Reconcile your accounts with bank and credit card statements each month. This helps identify discrepancies and keep your records accurate.

Step 2:

Track Expenses for Tax Purposes

- **Use Tax-Deductible Categories:** Mark relevant expense categories as "Tax-Related" to simplify tax preparation. Quicken allows you to generate tax reports that summarize all tax-deductible business expenses.

- **Generate Tax Reports:** At the end of the year, generate "Tax Summary" or "Schedule C" reports that detail your business income and expenses, making it easy to file taxes and maximize deductions.

How to Separate Personal and Business Accounts in Quicken to Ensure Accurate Financial Tracking

Separating personal and business finances is crucial for effectively managing your financial health and maintaining organized records. Using Quicken, you can easily keep your personal and business accounts distinct, allowing you to track income and expenses for each independently. This separation is not only vital for getting an accurate picture of your business's profitability but also makes tax preparation easier and minimizes the risk of errors or confusion.

Why Separate Personal and Business Accounts?

Separating personal and business accounts offers numerous benefits, including:

- **Accurate Financial Tracking:** Keeping personal and business transactions separate ensures that your financial records reflect the actual performance of your business without being influenced by personal expenses.
- **Simplified Tax Preparation:** Maintaining separate accounts helps you easily identify tax-deductible business expenses and avoid commingling of funds, which is crucial for preparing accurate tax returns.
- **Clear Financial Picture:** By separating your finances, you can gain a clear understanding of your business profitability, cash flow, and overall financial health without the noise of personal transactions.

Setting Up Separate Accounts in Quicken

The first step to separating your personal and business finances in Quicken is to create individual accounts for each. Quicken allows you to add multiple accounts and categorize them as either business or personal, ensuring a clean separation of financial data.

Step 1:

Create Personal Accounts

- **Add Personal Accounts:** In Quicken, click on "Tools > Add Account" and select the appropriate type of account for your personal finances, such as "Checking", "Savings", or "Credit Card".

- **Name the Account:** Provide clear names like "Personal Checking" or "Personal Credit Card" so you can easily distinguish them from business accounts.

Step 2:

Create Business Accounts

- **Add Business Accounts:** Repeat the steps to create separate business accounts. Under "Tools > Add Account", select the account type and categorize it as a business account.

- **Use Descriptive Names:** Name these accounts descriptively, such as "Business Checking" or "Business Credit Card," to differentiate them from personal accounts.

Categorizing Personal and Business Transactions

Accurately categorizing transactions is key to maintaining a clean separation between personal and business finances in Quicken. Proper categorization also helps when generating reports or calculating tax deductions.

Step 1:

Use Specific Categories

- **Create Custom Categories:** Quicken allows you to create custom categories to suit your specific needs. For example, for personal accounts, you may create categories like "Groceries", "Rent", or "Utilities". For business accounts, you might create categories like "Supplies", "Client Payments", and "Advertising".

- **Categorize Expenses and Income Correctly:** Ensure that all transactions are assigned to the appropriate category. Business expenses should be recorded under business categories, while personal expenses should go under personal categories. This practice keeps records organized and makes generating financial reports more effective.

Step 2:

Mark Business-Related Categories as Tax-Related

- Identify Tax-Deductible Categories: When creating categories for business transactions, mark them as "Tax-Related" in Quicken. This ensures that all deductible business expenses are tracked, simplifying tax filing at year-end.

- Use Tags for Additional Detail: Use tags to track specific projects or clients within your business. Tags allow you to group expenses related to a particular client or project, which can be useful for analysing profitability or generating reports.

Keeping Transactions Separate

Separating personal and business transactions in Quicken ensures that your financial records remain organized, and it helps you avoid inadvertently mixing up personal and business finances.

Step 1:

Enter Transactions in the Correct Account

- **Manually Add Transactions to the Right Account:** When adding new transactions, ensure they are entered in the correct account register—either personal or business. For example, if you use your business credit card to buy office supplies, record it in the "Business Credit Card" account register and assign the expense to a business-related category.

- **Download and Review Transactions:** If your accounts are linked to Quicken, transactions will automatically download. Carefully review these transactions to verify they are recorded in the correct account.

Step 2:

Avoid Mixing Personal and Business Funds

- **Use Separate Bank Accounts:** Always use separate bank accounts and credit cards for personal and business purposes. This makes it easier to track your spending and ensures that there is no crossover between personal and business finances.

- **Correct Misclassified Transactions:** If a transaction is mistakenly recorded in the wrong account or category, edit the entry to correct it. This prevents inaccuracies in your financial reports and keeps your records clean.

Generating Separate Reports for Personal and Business Accounts

Quickens reporting features allow you to generate separate financial reports for personal and business accounts, giving you clear insights into each area without interference from the other.

Step 1:

Generate Personal Reports

- **Navigate to Reports > Spending:** In the "Reports" section, select "Spending" to generate reports based on personal accounts. You can create reports such as "Spending by Category" or "Income and Expense" to review your personal finances.

- **Set Filters for Personal Accounts Only:** Filter the report to include only your personal accounts. This ensures the generated report reflects your personal spending and income, separate from any business transactions.

Step 2:

Generate Business Reports

- **Navigate to Reports > Business:** In the "Reports" section, select "Business" to create reports like "Profit and Loss", "Cash Flow", and "Invoices". These reports help you understand the financial health of your business.

- **Review Business Performance:** Reviewing business reports gives you insights into your company's performance, income, and expenses, helping you make data-driven decisions to improve profitability.

Generating Profit and Loss Reports in Quicken

Profit and Loss (P&L) reports, also known as income statements, are essential for understanding the financial health of a business. They summarize your income and expenses over a specific period, providing a clear picture of your profitability. Quicken simplifies the process of generating these reports, enabling you to analyze your business performance and make informed financial decisions.

What Is a Profit and Loss Report?

A Profit and Loss report displays your business income, expenses, and net profit or loss over a chosen period. It helps you:

- **Monitor Business Performance:** By comparing revenue and expenses, you can determine how well your business is doing.
- **Identify Cost-Saving Opportunities:** Reviewing your expenses lets you identify areas where you may be able to cut costs.
- **Plan for the Future:** Understanding your financial position helps you make strategic decisions about future investments or expansions.

Steps to Generate a Profit and Loss Report in Quicken

Step 1:

Access the Reports Menu

- Open Quicken and navigate to the "Reports" menu.

- Select "Business" or "Income & Expense" depending on the version of Quicken you are using.

Step 2:

Choose the Profit and Loss Report Option

- From the list of available reports, select "Profit and Loss" or "Income Statement".
- If your version of Quicken doesn't directly show this option, it may be listed under a broader category such as "Business Reports".

Step 3:

Customize the Report Settings

- **Select the Date Range:** Choose the period you want the report to cover (e.g., monthly, quarterly, annually).
- **Filter by Accounts:** Make sure to select only your business accounts so that the report accurately reflects your business income and expenses. You can choose multiple accounts if necessary.
- **Categories:** Ensure that all relevant categories are included. You can customize the report to focus on specific categories of income or expenses if you need more detailed analysis.
- **Additional Filters:** If you have tags or classes, use them to filter the report further, helping you to focus on specific projects or business units.

Step 4:

Generate and Review the Report

- Click "Generate" or "Create Report" after setting your preferences. Quicken will process the data and display your Profit and Loss report.

- **Review the Summary:** The report will typically show a summary of your total income, total expenses, and net profit or loss. Make sure everything looks correct.

- **Examine Detailed Sections:** Look at the detailed breakdown of income and expenses to understand what drives your business's profitability.

Step 5:

Save or Export the Report

- **Save the Report:** If you want to keep the report for future reference, you can save it within Quicken. This is helpful for tracking your financial performance over time.

- **Export for Further Analysis:** Quicken allows you to export reports in various formats, including "PDF" and "Excel". Exporting to Excel is useful if you need to manipulate the data further or present it in a customized format.

- **Print the Report:** You can also print the report directly if you need a hard copy for meetings or record-keeping.

Understanding the Profit and Loss Report Sections

A typical Profit and Loss report in Quicken will have the following sections:

- **Income:** Lists all revenue sources, including sales, services, and other income streams. Reviewing this section helps you understand which areas generate the most revenue.

- **Expenses:** Breaks down all costs, including operating expenses, administrative costs, and other expenditures. Analysing expenses can help you identify where you can reduce costs.
- **Net Profit/Loss:** Shows the difference between total income and total expenses, indicating whether your business made a profit or incurred a loss over the selected period.

Understanding each section will allow you to gain insights into your business performance and make informed decisions. For instance, a high expense in a particular category may indicate that cost-cutting measures are needed.

Tips for Effective Profit and Loss Reporting in Quicken

- **Regularly Update Your Data:** Make sure to update your income and expense transactions in Quicken regularly so that your reports are always accurate and up to date.
- **Reconcile Your Accounts:** Before generating your Profit and Loss report, reconcile your accounts to ensure that all transactions have been correctly recorded.
- **Review Regularly:** Run Profit and Loss reports periodically (e.g., monthly or quarterly) to monitor your business performance. Regular review helps you catch any discrepancies early and make necessary adjustments.

Tracking Your Revenue, Expenses, and Overall Business Health Using Quicken

Effective financial tracking is vital for any business, as it helps monitor revenue, manage expenses, and maintain a clear understanding of overall business health. Quicken provides robust tools that simplify this process, enabling business owners to make informed decisions based on accurate financial data.

Monitoring Revenue

Revenue tracking is essential to understand how much money your business is generating. With Quicken, you can:

- **Link Business Accounts:** Connect your bank accounts, credit cards, and payment processors to Quicken. This allows for automatic syncing of income, ensuring you have up-to-date information on all money coming into the business.

- **Record Sales and Income:** Manually input any income that isn't automatically synced, such as cash sales or payments received by check. This keeps your revenue records accurate.

- **Categorize Income Sources:** Use categories to differentiate between various income streams. For instance, if your business has multiple services or products, you can categorize them separately to analyse which revenue sources are the most profitable.

Managing Expenses

Tracking expenses is equally important as monitoring revenue, as it helps you control costs and improve profitability. With Quicken, you can:

- **Automate Expense Tracking:** By linking your business bank accounts and credit cards, Quicken can automatically pull in expenses, reducing the need for manual data entry.

- **Categorize Expenditures:** Create specific categories for different types of expenses, such as utilities, rent, salaries, office supplies, and marketing. This helps you identify where your money is going and spot potential areas for cost reduction.

- **Set Spending Limits:** Use Quickens budgeting feature to set monthly spending limits for each expense category. The software will alert you if you are approaching or exceeding these limits, helping you stay on track.

Gaining a Holistic View of Business Health

Understanding the overall health of your business requires a balance between tracking revenue, managing expenses, and analysing profitability. Quicken provides tools to integrate these aspects, giving you a clear view of your business's financial condition.

- **Net Profit Analysis:** By comparing your total revenue to your total expenses, Quicken calculates your net profit, showing whether your business is making money or losing it. Regularly reviewing this information helps ensure your business remains financially sustainable.

- **Cash Flow Management:** Use Quickens cash flow reports to see how money moves in and out of your business. Effective cash flow management helps prevent liquidity issues, ensuring you always have enough funds to cover essential expenses.

- **Net Worth Tracking:** Quicken can also track your business's net worth by summarizing all assets (e.g., cash, accounts receivable, equipment) and liabilities (e.g., loans, debts). This gives you a comprehensive view of your business's financial position.

Managing Payroll and Contractor Payments Using Quicken

Effective payroll and contractor management are essential for maintaining smooth business operations and ensuring your team gets paid accurately and on time. Quicken can simplify these tasks, providing tools to track salaries, wages, and contractor payments seamlessly. Here's how you can utilize Quicken to manage payroll and handle payments for contractors:

1. Setting Up Payroll in Quicken

Managing payroll begins with setting up the necessary accounts and categories to track salaries, taxes, and other deductions. While Quicken doesn't have a built-in payroll processing feature like dedicated payroll software, it can still be used to manage and track payroll information efficiently.

- **Create a Payroll Expense Category:** Start by setting up a specific category for payroll expenses. This helps you separate employee salaries from other business costs, making it easier to track your total payroll expenditures.

- **Add Employee Details:** Manually record information for each employee, including name, salary, pay frequency (weekly, bi-weekly, monthly), and any additional benefits or deductions (such as health insurance, retirement contributions, or tax withholding).

- **Track Payroll Deductions:** For accurate payroll tracking, ensure your account for various deductions and benefits. Create subcategories under payroll expenses for items like taxes, insurance, and other deductions to get a detailed view of your payroll costs.

2. Recording Payroll Transactions

Once your payroll is set up, you'll need to regularly input payroll transactions to reflect payments made to employees. Here's how to do it:

- **Manual Payroll Entry:** Each time you run payroll, enter the total amount paid to each employee, including a breakdown of gross pay, deductions, and net pay. This can be done by adding a new transaction in Quicken under the payroll expense category.

- **Use Split Transactions:** To account for multiple components in a single payroll payment (e.g., gross pay, federal tax, state tax, health insurance), use Quickens split transaction feature. This lets you divide a single payment into several parts, ensuring each aspect of the payroll is recorded accurately.

3. Managing Contractor Payments

Unlike employees, contractors are typically paid based on invoices or agreed-upon rates for specific projects. Managing contractor payments in Quicken is straightforward:

- **Create a Contractor Payment Category:** Similar to payroll, create a separate category specifically for contractor payments. This helps keep your contractor costs distinct from other business expenses.

- **Record Payments to Contractors:** Whenever you make a payment to a contractor, log it in Quicken by entering a transaction under the contractor payment category. Include details such as the contractor's name, project description, and payment amount.

- **Track Contractor Expenses by Project:** If you hire contractors for different projects, you can set up separate subcategories or use tags to track expenses by project. This is useful for evaluating the cost-effectiveness of each project and understanding where your money is going.

4. Automating Payroll and Contractor Payments

To make managing payroll and contractor payments easier, consider automating some processes. Although Quicken doesn't process payroll, it can integrate with payroll software or services that do:

- **Link Bank Accounts for Automated Updates:** By linking your business bank accounts to Quicken, any payments you make to employees or contractors will be automatically synced. This reduces the need for manual entry and ensures your records stay accurate.

- **Integration with Payroll Services:** If you use a dedicated payroll service (like ADP, Gusto, or Paychex), you can export payroll data from that service and import it into Quicken. This lets you manage payroll data in Quicken without having to enter everything manually.

5. Generating Payroll and Contractor Payment Reports

Quickens reporting features can be used to track payroll expenses and contractor payments over time. These reports help you understand the overall cost of labor, compare expenses month-to-month, and ensure that all payments are accurately recorded.

- **Payroll Expense Reports:** Generate payroll expense reports to see how much you're spending on employee salaries, taxes, and benefits. These reports can also help with budgeting and forecasting, enabling you to plan for future payroll needs.

- **Contractor Expense Reports:** Quicken can also create reports summarizing how much you've paid to contractors. You can filter these reports by contractor name, project, or time period, giving you insights into your contractor expenses

6. Tax Compliance for Payroll and Contractors

Properly managing payroll and contractor payments is not just about paying people on time; it also involves staying compliant with tax regulations:

- **Track Payroll Taxes:** Set up categories for different types of payroll taxes (federal, state, local) and ensure you regularly record these payments. Quicken can help you monitor your tax liabilities and prepare for quarterly or annual tax filings.

- **Issue 1099s for Contractors:** If you pay contractors, you'll need to issue 1099 forms for tax purposes. Quicken can help you track all payments made to each contractor, making it easier to generate accurate 1099s when tax season comes around.

7. **Best Practices for Managing Payroll and Contractor Payments with Quicken**

- **Regularly Reconcile Accounts:** Ensure that your Quicken records match your bank statements. Reconciling accounts monthly can help you catch any discrepancies early, reducing the risk of errors.

- **Maintain Accurate Records:** Make sure to input all payroll and contractor payments as soon as they are made. Keeping accurate records will save you time during tax season and make it easier to generate reports.

- **Backup Your Data:** Regularly back up your Quicken data to avoid losing critical financial information. This is especially important for payroll records, as they may be required for tax compliance and audits.

Managing payroll and contractor payments doesn't have to be a complicated process. With Quicken, you can set up categories for payroll and contractor expenses, automate payment tracking, and generate insightful reports. By integrating Quicken with other payroll services, you can streamline your payroll management and ensure all payments are accurately recorded. Regularly reviewing payroll and contractor expense reports can help you control labour costs, budget more effectively, and keep your business running smoothly.

Tracking Payments for Employees and Freelancers Using Quicken

Efficiently tracking payments for both employees and freelancers is crucial for accurate financial management and budgeting. Quicken offers tools to help you monitor payments, organize records, and ensure that every transaction is properly accounted for. Here's how to use Quicken to manage payments for your team, whether they are full-time employees or freelance contractors.

Setting Up Payment Categories

The first step in tracking payments is to set up distinct categories for employees and freelancers. This will help you differentiate between the two and allow for better financial analysis.

- **Employee Payments:** Create a category specifically for employee salaries and wages. This category can include subcategories for various deductions, such as taxes, insurance, and retirement contributions. By breaking down these payments, you'll get a clear view of your payroll expenses.
- **Freelancer Payments:** Similarly, set up a category for freelance or contract payments. You can organize this further by project or individual freelancer, depending on your business needs. This ensures all freelance payments are easily identifiable and traceable.

Recording Payments to Employees

Tracking employee payments involves regularly entering salary, wages, and other related expenses in Quicken. Even though Quicken doesn't process payroll directly, it can help you maintain a clear record of all payments made to employees.

- **Manual Entry of Payroll:** Each time you process payroll, input the total payment amount, along with a breakdown of deductions and net pay. Using the "split transaction" feature can be helpful here, allowing you to record each component (e.g., gross pay, taxes, benefits) within a single entry.
- **Recurring Payroll Transactions:** If employees are paid on a regular schedule, set up recurring transactions. This will automatically log payments each pay period, reducing the need for manual entry and minimizing errors.

Tracking Payments to Freelancers

Unlike employees, freelancers are typically paid based on invoices or agreed rates. Quicken allows you to track these payments separately and organize them based on individual projects or clients.

- **Create Entries for Each Payment:** When paying a freelancer, add a new transaction under the freelance payment category. Include relevant details such as the freelancer's name, project, and invoice number, which can be helpful for reference during audits or end-of-year reviews.
- **Use Tags for Better Tracking:** If you work with multiple freelancers, you can use tags to categorize payments by project, department, or client. This makes it easier to see how much you are spending on specific projects or teams.

Linking Bank Accounts for Automatic Updates

For businesses that handle numerous transactions, manually entering each payment can be time-consuming. By linking your business bank account to Quicken, you can automate the process of tracking payments.

- **Automatic Transaction Import:** Once your bank account is linked, Quicken will import all transactions directly from your bank. You can then categorize each payment as either an employee salary or a freelance invoice, streamlining the process and ensuring no payments are missed.

- **Reconcile Transactions Regularly:** Periodically reconciling your accounts ensures that the information in Quicken matches your bank statements. This helps catch any discrepancies, such as missed payments or incorrect amounts, and keeps your financial records accurate.

Generating Payment Reports

Quickens reporting features allow you to generate detailed reports on payments made to employees and freelancers. This provides insights into where your money is going and helps with budgeting and forecasting.

- **Payroll Reports:** Create reports to show how much you've spent on salaries, taxes, and benefits over a specific period. These reports can be customized to highlight particular expenses, making it easy to analyse your total payroll costs.

- **Freelance Payment Reports:** You can also generate reports to track freelance expenses by individual contractor, project, or time frame. This is especially useful for businesses that rely on freelancers for various tasks, as it allows you to see how much you are spending on external talent.

CHAPTER TEN: ADVANCED TIPS AND TROUBLESHOOTING GUIDE

While Quicken is an intuitive tool designed to simplify your financial management, mastering its full potential can unlock even greater efficiency and accuracy in managing your finances. In this section, we'll explore advanced tips that can take your Quicken skills to the next level, from fine-tuning your budgeting categories to leveraging powerful reports that give you deeper insights into your financial habits. Even the most experienced Quicken users occasionally encounter issues or need help troubleshooting specific functions. Whether you're facing syncing errors, issues with bank connections, or just need advice on how to optimize your workflow, this section offers practical solutions to common challenges. These advanced tips and troubleshooting techniques ensure that you can use Quicken to its full capacity, making it a reliable tool for managing your finances and achieving your financial goals.

Common Issues and How to Resolve Them in Quicken

While Quicken is a powerful tool, like any software, you may encounter occasional issues. Whether it's syncing problems, missing transactions, or errors with financial data, these common challenges can disrupt your workflow. In this section, we'll address some of the most frequent issues users face and provide clear, step-by-step solutions to help you resolve them quickly. With these tips, you'll be able to troubleshoot efficiently and get back to managing your finances with ease. Even with a user-friendly interface, you might occasionally encounter issues while using

Quicken. Understanding common problems and how to resolve them can help maintain a seamless experience. Below are some typical issues users face, along with step-by-step solutions to address them.

Difficulty Connecting to Bank Accounts

Problem: Users often experience challenges when trying to link their bank accounts to Quicken. These issues can arise due to incorrect login information, changes in the bank's website, or connectivity problems.

Solution:

- **Check Login Credentials:** Ensure that you are entering the correct username and password for your bank account. If you have recently changed your credentials, update them in Quicken as well.

- **Verify Bank's Online Services:** Sometimes, the issue may be on the bank's side. Check if your bank is experiencing downtime or has made changes to its online services.

- **Refresh Bank Connection:** Go to the account that's experiencing the issue, right-click on it, and select "Update Now." Follow the prompts to reconnect your bank account.

- **Disable and Re-enable the Account:** If refreshing does not work, you can try disconnecting the account and then linking it again. Go to "Account Settings," select "Online Services," and click "Deactivate." Afterward, re-link the account to see if the issue is resolved.

Duplicate Transactions

Problem: Duplicate transactions can clutter your records and make it difficult to accurately track your finances. This issue often occurs when transactions are imported multiple times or if the same account is linked more than once.

Solution:

- **Remove Duplicates Manually:** Go through your account register and identify any duplicates. Right-click on the duplicated transaction and choose "Delete" to remove it.

- **Check Your Download Settings:** Adjust your settings to avoid downloading transactions that have already been imported. This can be done in the "Preferences" menu, under "Download Transactions."

- **Disable and Reconnect Your Account:** If the problem persists, disconnect your account from online services and then reconnect. This can reset the transaction download and clear any underlying issues.

Incorrect Balance After Reconciliation

Problem: Sometimes, your account balance in Quicken may not match the actual balance in your bank account, even after reconciling your transactions. This discrepancy can occur if transactions are missing or incorrectly categorized.

Solution:

- **Check for Missing Transactions:** Compare your Quicken register with your bank statement to identify any missing transactions. Add these manually if necessary.

- **Review Reconciled Transactions:** Make sure all transactions have been correctly reconciled. If any are missing a reconciliation checkmark, go through the process of reconciling them again.

- **Adjust Starting Balance:** Verify that the starting balance in Quicken matches your bank statement. If there's a discrepancy, manually adjust the starting balance to reflect the correct amount.

Performance Issues or Crashes

Problem: Quicken may occasionally run slowly or crash, particularly when dealing with large databases or outdated software.

Solution:

- **Update Quicken Software:** Make sure you are using the latest version of Quicken. Software updates often include fixes for known issues, which can help improve performance.

- **Reduce File Size:** If your Quicken file has become too large, it can slow down the program. Archive older data or delete unnecessary accounts to reduce the file size.

- **Run Quicken File Validation:** Quicken has a built-in tool to check for file errors. Go to "File," select "File Operations," and choose "Validate and Repair." This can help identify and fix any issues within your Quicken data file.

- **Reinstall Quicken:** If performance issues persist, try uninstalling and reinstalling the software. Make sure to back up your data before doing this.

Issues with Backups and Restoring Files

Problem: Users sometimes face difficulties backing up their Quicken files or restoring data from a backup. This can be especially frustrating if you rely on backups for safeguarding your financial information.

Solution:

- **Check Backup Settings:** Make sure Quicken is set to automatically back up your files. You can find this option in the "Backup and Restore" settings under "Preferences."

- **Backup Files Manually:** If automatic backups are not working, create a manual backup by going to "File" and selecting "Backup and Restore" > "Backup Quicken File." Save the file to a secure location, such as an external drive or cloud storage.

- **Use the Correct File Format When Restoring:** Ensure that you are restoring a .QDF (Quicken Data File) or .QFX (Quicken Financial Exchange) file. Other file types might not be compatible, leading to restoration issues.

- Verify Backup File Integrity: Sometimes, a backup file may become corrupted. If you encounter issues while restoring, try using a different backup file or create a new backup.

Syncing Issues with Mobile App

Problem: Syncing data between the desktop version of Quicken and the mobile app can sometimes be inconsistent, causing discrepancies in your accounts.

Solution:

- **Verify Internet Connection:** Ensure that both your computer and mobile device have a stable internet connection. Syncing issues can occur if there are interruptions in the connection.

- **Update Both Applications:** Make sure you have the latest version of both the desktop software and the mobile app. Updates often resolve syncing issues.

- **Reset Cloud Sync Data:** Go to Quickens desktop version, select "Edit," and then "Preferences." Under "Quicken ID, Sync & Alerts," choose "Reset your cloud data." This can help clear any syncing problems and refresh the data on your mobile app.

Bank Syncing Problems — How to Manually Refresh or Re-Sync Accounts

One common issue that Quicken users encounter is trouble syncing their bank accounts. This problem can arise due to various reasons, such as changes on the bank's website, connectivity issues, or outdated credentials. Fortunately, there are ways to manually refresh or re-sync your accounts to get things back on track.

Manually Refresh Bank Accounts

If your bank transactions are not syncing correctly, manually refreshing the connection can help:

- **Step 1:** Open Quicken and navigate to the account that is having syncing issues.

- **Step 2:** Right-click on the account name in the sidebar.

- **Step 3:** Select "Update Now" from the menu. This will prompt Quicken to reconnect to your bank and attempt to download any missing transactions.
- **Step 4:** Follow any prompts that ask you to verify your bank credentials. Make sure the username and password are accurate and up to date.

Re-Sync the Account

If refreshing doesn't solve the issue, re-syncing the account may be necessary. Re-syncing involves disconnecting and reconnecting your bank account:

- **Step 1:** Go to the affected account and click on "Account Settings."
- **Step 2:** Under the "Online Services" tab, click "Deactivate." This will disconnect your account from online syncing.
- **Step 3:** After deactivating, click "Set Up Now" or "Add Account" to reconnect the bank account. Follow the prompts to link your account once more.
- **Step 4:** Ensure that the correct credentials are entered, and allow Quicken to download and sync all available transactions.

Update Your Bank Credentials

Sometimes, syncing issues occur if your bank credentials have changed. If you recently updated your bank's password or username, be sure to update it in Quicken:

- **Step 1:** Select the account with syncing problems and go to "Account Settings."
- **Step 2:** Navigate to the "Online Services" tab.
- **Step 3:** Click "Edit Login Information" and enter your new username and password.

- **Step 4:** Confirm the details and allow Quicken to reconnect to your bank.

Check for Bank Connectivity Issues

If your bank is experiencing technical difficulties or maintenance, it may cause temporary syncing problems in Quicken. You can check your bank's website for updates on their online services. If the issue is from their end, syncing should resume once their services are restored.

Tips to Avoid Future Syncing Issues

- **Keep Your Quicken Software Updated:** Regular updates can help fix bugs that may cause syncing issues. Make sure you are using the latest version of Quicken.

- **Verify Internet Connection:** A stable internet connection is essential for syncing bank accounts. Ensure you have a reliable connection whenever you update your accounts.

- **Clear Sync Data Occasionally:** Resetting cloud sync data periodically can prevent syncing errors. This option is available in Quickens preferences menu under "Quicken ID, Sync & Alerts."

By following these steps, you can effectively refresh or re-sync your Quicken accounts and maintain accurate financial tracking.

Duplicate Transactions — How to Merge or Delete Duplicates

Duplicate transactions can create confusion and make it difficult to get an accurate picture of your finances in Quicken. Duplicates may occur due to multiple downloads from the bank, manual entry errors, or syncing issues. Fortunately, Quicken provides straightforward methods to identify, merge, or delete these duplicates to maintain clean and organized records.

Identifying Duplicate Transactions

Before merging or deleting duplicates, it's important to identify them:

- **Step 1:** Go to the account register where you suspect duplicates may be present.

- **Step 2:** Sort the transactions by "Date" or "Amount" to make it easier to spot duplicates. Sorting can help you quickly locate similar transactions that were recorded more than once.

- **Step 3:** Review the details of the suspected duplicate entries, including the date, amount, and payee information. Confirm that they represent the same transaction before taking further action.

Merging Duplicate Transactions

If you find two entries for the same transaction but want to retain the information from both (such as notes, tags, or categories), you can merge them:

- **Step 1:** Highlight the two duplicate transactions by clicking on them while holding down the "Ctrl" (Windows) or "Command" (Mac) key.

- **Step 2:** Right-click on one of the selected transactions and choose "Merge Transactions" from the menu.

- **Step 3:** Quicken will combine the details from both entries into a single transaction, preserving key information and eliminating the duplicate.

Deleting Duplicate Transactions

If merging isn't necessary and you simply want to remove the extra transaction:

- **Step 1:** Select the duplicate transaction that you wish to delete. Make sure you've reviewed it carefully to confirm that it is truly a duplicate.

- **Step 2:** Right-click on the transaction and choose "Delete" from the drop-down menu.

- **Step 3:** Quicken may prompt you to confirm the deletion. Click "Yes" to proceed.

- **Step 4:** If you have multiple duplicates, repeat the process until all unnecessary entries are removed.

Adjusting Download Settings to Prevent Duplicates

Preventing duplicates from appearing in the first place can save time:

- **Step 1:** Go to "Edit" (Windows) or "Quicken" (Mac) and select "Preferences."

- **Step 2:** Navigate to "Download Transactions" and review the settings. Ensure that the "Automatically Add to Register" option is disabled, so that you can review transactions before they are added.

- **Step 3:** Use Quickens "Match Transactions" feature, which can detect duplicates when importing new entries from your bank and help prevent them from being added again.

Resetting Your Online Connection

If you frequently encounter duplicates due to issues with online syncing, consider resetting your connection:

- **Step 1:** Go to "Account Settings" for the affected account.

- **Step 2:** Under "Online Services," click "Deactivate." This will disconnect the account from online services, which can help clear any syncing errors causing duplicates.

- **Step 3:** After deactivating, reconnect the account by selecting "Set Up Now" or "Add Account," and follow the prompts to re-establish the online connection.

Tips to Keep Your Quicken Register Clean

A clean and organized Quicken register is essential for accurate financial tracking and smooth budgeting. Regularly updating your transactions and categorizing expenses can help prevent errors and ensure that your financial records remain precise. In this section, we'll share practical tips to help you maintain a tidy Quicken register, reduce discrepancies, and keep your financial data in top shape, making it easier to track spending and plan ahead.

- **Regularly Review Transactions:** Make it a habit to review your transactions regularly to catch any duplicates early.

- **Back Up Your Data:** Before making bulk changes, ensure that your data is backed up so that you can restore it if necessary.

- **Manually Enter Recurring Transactions:** If certain transactions appear as duplicates often, consider entering them manually rather than relying on automatic downloads.

Effectively managing duplicates in Quicken ensures that your financial records remain clear, accurate, and easy to understand. By regularly checking for duplicates and using Quickens built-in tools to merge or delete them, you can maintain a clean register and avoid confusion when reviewing your finances.

Using Advanced Features in Quicken

Quicken is not just a basic budgeting tool; it also offers advanced features designed to enhance your financial management experience. By leveraging these functionalities, you can gain deeper insights into your financial health, streamline your processes, and improve your overall efficiency. This section will explore several key advanced features in Quicken and how to effectively use them.

Customizing Your Dashboard

The dashboard is your central hub in Quicken, providing an overview of your financial situation. You can customize it to display the information that matters most to you:

- **Step 1:** Open Quicken and navigate to the "Dashboard" section.
- **Step 2:** Click on "Customize" in the upper right corner of the dashboard. This option allows you to select which widgets to display.
- **Step 3:** Choose from various widgets such as "Net Worth," "Spending Trends," and "Investment Performance." Drag and drop the widgets to rearrange them according to your preferences.
- **Step 4:** Once you're satisfied with your layout, save the changes. This personalized dashboard will provide quick access to the most relevant information.

Creating Custom Categories

Quicken allows you to create custom categories tailored to your specific financial needs, giving you greater control over your budgeting:

- **Step 1:** Go to the "Tools" menu and select "Category List."
- **Step 2:** Click "New Category" to create a category that reflects your unique spending habits, such as "Travel," "Home Renovations," or "Education."
- **Step 3:** Assign the new category a parent category if desired, and customize the colour for easier identification.
- Step 4: Use this custom category to track relevant transactions and gain better insights into your spending patterns.

Setting Up Alerts and Reminders

Keeping track of bills and financial deadlines is crucial for maintaining a healthy financial life. Quickens alerts and reminders can help ensure that you never miss a payment:

- **Step 1:** Navigate to the "Reminders" section in Quicken.

- **Step 2:** Click "Add Reminder" and select the type of reminder you want to set up, such as "Bill Reminder" or "Transfer Reminder."

- **Step 3:** Fill out the necessary details, including the amount, due date, and frequency (e.g., monthly, quarterly).

- **Step 4:** Choose how you would like to be notified—via email, pop-up, or a mobile alert. Save the reminder, and Quicken will notify you as your payment dates approach.

Utilizing Investment Tools

Quicken provides several powerful investment tracking features to help you manage your portfolio effectively:

- **Step 1:** Link your investment accounts to Quicken to automatically download transaction data and current values.

- **Step 2:** Use the "Investment Performance" report to assess how your portfolio is doing over time. You can view gains, losses, and the overall performance of individual investments.

- **Step 3:** Create custom reports that focus on specific aspects of your investments, such as "Asset Allocation" or "Investment Income." To do this, go to the "Reports" menu, select "Investment," and customize the report parameters according to your needs.

Generating Advanced Reports

Quicken offers robust reporting features that allow you to analyse your financial data in various ways:

- **Step 1:** Click on the "Reports" menu to view the different report types available, including "Income," "Expenses," and "Cash Flow."

- **Step 2:** Choose a report type and click on "Customize" to tailor the report to your specific needs. You can filter by date ranges, categories, and accounts.

- **Step 3:** Save your customized report settings for future use. You can also export reports to formats like PDF or Excel for easy sharing or further analysis.

Syncing with Mobile Devices

Quicken offers a mobile app that syncs with your desktop software, allowing you to manage your finances on the go:

- **Step 1:** Download the Quicken mobile app from your device's app store and log in using your Quicken ID.

- **Step 2:** Enable syncing in the desktop version of Quicken by navigating to "Quicken ID, Sync & Alerts" in preferences and turning on the sync feature.

- **Step 3:** Use the mobile app to view transactions, add expenses, and check your financial status from anywhere. All changes made in the app will automatically sync with your desktop version.

Backing Up Your Data Regularly Using the File > Backup Feature

One of the most crucial steps in maintaining your financial records in Quicken is ensuring that your data is backed up regularly. Unexpected events, such as computer malfunctions, software crashes, or accidental deletions, can lead to the loss of vital financial information. To safeguard your data, Quicken provides an easy-to-use backup feature that allows you to create secure copies of your financial files. Here's how to effectively back up your data using the "File > Backup" feature.

Understanding the Importance of Backing Up

Backing up your Quicken data is essential for several reasons:

- **Protection Against Data Loss:** Regular backups protect your financial records from unforeseen issues, such as hardware failures or software errors.
- **Recovery from Mistakes:** If you accidentally delete a transaction or make an error in your file, having a backup allows you to restore your data to a previous state.
- **Peace of Mind:** Knowing that your financial information is secure helps you manage your finances with confidence

Initiating the Backup Process

To back up your data in Quicken, follow these straightforward steps:

- **Step 1:** Open Quicken on your computer.
- **Step 2:** Go to the "File" menu located at the top left corner of the screen.
- Step 3: Select "Backup" from the dropdown menu. This action will open the backup dialog box.

Choosing Your Backup Location

When backing up your data, you'll need to choose a safe location to save the backup file:

- **Step 4:** In the backup dialog box, you will see the default backup location. You can choose to keep it there or select a different folder by clicking on the "Browse" button.
- Step 5: It's advisable to select an external drive, USB flash drive, or cloud storage option (like Google Drive or Dropbox) for an extra layer of protection. This way, your data remains safe even if your computer encounters issues.

Naming Your Backup File

Quicken allows you to customize the name of your backup file to make it easier to identify later:

- **Step 6:** You can rename the backup file if desired. A good practice is to include the date in the filename (e.g., "QuickenBackup_October2024.qdf") to help track when the backup was created.

Completing the Backup

Once you have selected the location and named the file, you can complete the backup process:

- **Step 7:** Click the "OK" button to initiate the backup. Quicken will create a backup of your data, which may take a few moments depending on the size of your file.

- **Step 8:** After the backup is complete, a confirmation message will appear, indicating that your data has been successfully backed up.

Establishing a Backup Routine

To ensure your financial data remains secure, it's important to establish a regular backup routine:

- **Frequency:** Aim to back up your data at least once a week or after making significant changes, such as entering a large number of transactions or updating your investment accounts.

- **Automated Backups:** Consider setting a reminder on your calendar or using a task management app to prompt you for backups. Some users prefer to do this at the beginning or end of the week.

Restoring Data from Backup

In case you need to restore your data from a backup, follow these steps:

- **Step 9:** Go to the "File" menu again.

- **Step 10:** Select "Restore Backup" and navigate to the location where your backup file is stored.

- **Step 11:** Choose the backup file you wish to restore and click "Open." Quicken will prompt you to confirm that you want to replace the current data with the backup data.

Restoring Your Data if Needed and Ensuring Data Security with Encryption Options

In the digital age, safeguarding your financial data is crucial. Quicken provides tools not only for backing up your data but also for restoring it when necessary. Moreover, it offers encryption options to enhance the security of your sensitive information. This guide will walk you through the process of restoring your Quicken data and implementing encryption for data security.

Understanding the Need for Data Restoration

There are several reasons you might need to restore your Quicken data:

- **Accidental Deletion:** You may inadvertently delete important transactions or accounts.

- **Software Issues:** A software crash or error could corrupt your Quicken file.

- **Device Failure:** Hardware failures or data corruption can necessitate a restoration from a backup.

Restoring Your Quicken Data

If you find yourself in a situation where you need to restore your Quicken data, follow these steps:

- **Step 1:** Open Quicken on your computer.
- **Step 2:** Go to the "File" menu located at the top left corner of the screen.
- **Step 3:** Select "Restore Backup." This option will allow you to access your backup files.
- **Step 4:** Navigate to the folder where your backup file is stored. If you followed best practices, this file should be named with a date for easy identification.
- **Step 5:** Select the backup file you want to restore and click "Open."
- **Step 6:** Quicken will prompt you to confirm that you want to overwrite the existing data with the backup. Carefully read the prompt to ensure you understand that this action cannot be undone. If you're ready, confirm the restoration.
- **Step 7:** After the restoration process is complete, review your financial data to ensure everything is intact and accurate.

Ensuring Data Security with Encryption Options

In addition to regular backups and restoration, securing your financial data is paramount. Quicken offers encryption options that provide an added layer of security, protecting your sensitive information from unauthorized access.

- **What is Encryption?** Encryption transforms your data into a secure format that can only be accessed or read by individuals with the correct decryption key or password. This process ensures that even if someone gains access to your files, they cannot read your sensitive information without the appropriate credentials.

Enabling Encryption in Quicken

To secure your Quicken data through encryption, follow these steps:

- **Step 1:** Open Quicken and navigate to the "Edit" menu.
- **Step 2:** Select "Preferences" from the dropdown list.
- **Step 3:** In the Preferences window, click on "Password" or "Security," depending on your version of Quicken.
- **Step 4:** Look for an option labelled "Enable Password Protection" or "Encrypt Data." Check the box to enable this feature.
- **Step 5:** Create a strong password that you will use to access your data. Make sure it includes a mix of letters, numbers, and special characters to enhance security.
- **Step 6:** Save your changes and exit the Preferences window. Quicken will now encrypt your data, requiring your password to access the file in the future.

Best Practices for Data Security

While Quickens encryption features enhance data security, following these best practices can further protect your financial information:

- **Use Strong Passwords:** Ensure your Quicken password is unique and complex and change it regularly.

- **Keep Software Updated:** Regularly update your Quicken software to benefit from the latest security features and patches.

- **Enable Two-Factor Authentication:** If available, enable two-factor authentication for an added layer of security.

- **Store Backups Securely:** Ensure that your backup files are stored in secure locations, such as an encrypted external drive or a reputable cloud storage service with encryption capabilities.

CONCLUSION

Best wishes! You've made it to the conclusion of this guide, and you're well on your way to learning Quicken and changing the way you handle your money. Whether you're tracking personal costs, running a small business, or budgeting for the future, the tools and ideas in this book will help you take control of your financial situation. At the beginning of this trip, you may have felt overwhelmed by the prospect of arranging your finances and using software such as Quicken. But now you know how to set up your Quicken account, track your income and expenses, create intelligent reports, and troubleshoot frequent errors. You've unlocked powerful features like budgeting, investment monitoring, and tax preparation, which will make money management easier and more efficient. We appreciate you taking the time to read this book and commit to improving your financial management skills. We believe that by using what you've learned here, you'll put yourself up for financial success. The road does not end here; it is simply the start of a more organized, stress-free, and financially empowered life. If this book has benefited you, we would appreciate it if you could give an honest review. Your opinion is really valuable to us since it not only helps us improve, but it also helps future readers who are just getting started with Quicken. Your review may inspire others to take control of their finances and go on the path to financial independence. Thank you again for your confidence and commitment to your financial future. We wish you all the best as you continue to use Quicken to simplify your finances and achieve your objectives. We are thrilled for you and can't wait to hear about your successes!